The Custom House and Town Beam, Poole.

Shire County Guide 9

DORSET

Peter Stanier

Shire Publicatior

D1285577

CONTENTS

Copyright © 1986 by Peter Stanier. First published 1986; second edition 1990. Shire County Guide 9. ISBN 0 7478 0049 9. All rights reserved. No part of this publication may be reproduced or transmitted in any form or by any means, electronic or mechanical, including photocopy, recording, or any information storage and retrieval system, without permission in writing from the publishers, Shire Publications Ltd, Cromwell House, Church Street, Princes Risborough, Aylesbury, Bucks HP17 9AJ, UK.

Set in 8 point Times roman and printed in Great Britain by C.I. Thomas & Sons (Haverfordwest) Ltd, Press Buildings, Merlins Bridge, Haverfordwest, Dyfed.

British Library Cataloguing in Publication Data available.

ACKNOWLEDGEMENTS

Photographs on the following pages are acknowledged to: Janice Johns, pages 20, 32, 38 (right); Cadbury Lamb, cover and pages 9, 19, 21, 22, 23, 26, 27, 28, 29, 40, 42, 45, 50, 56, 57, 58, 61, 62 (left). All other photographs are by the author. The map on pages 66-7 is by Mr D. R. Darton. The publishers wish to acknowledge the assistance of Mr R. N. R. Peers, Curator and Secretary of the Dorset Natural History and Archaeological Society.

COVER: *Gold Hill is a picturesque cobbled street in Shaftesbury.*

BELOW: *Weymouth is both a resort and a ferry port.*

The village pond at Ashmore may date back to Romano-British times.

1
The Dorset scene

Dorset is a rural county of great beauty and variety, especially along its coast. Inland, the scenery is less well known to the tourist, but there are many dramatic views and unspoilt farming villages to be discovered. The placenames — like Melbury Bubb, Nether Cerne, Rampisham or Toller Porcorum — are evocative of deepest Dorset. Geologically, the county is young, with mostly Jurassic and Cretaceous rocks, and more recent sands in the south-east. Distinct regions can be recognised where the underlying rocks have influenced the landscape, and consequently man's use of its resources. The rural nature of Dorset has ensured the survival of a great heritage, steeped in history.

While most evidence for earlier man is confined to the coast and river valleys, the chalk downs were being settled and farmed by neolithic times. The chalklands of central Dorset are rich in monuments of the neolithic, bronze and iron ages, suggesting that the prehistoric population was high in these parts. The Romans built a town at Dorchester, and roads, forts and villas have been discovered throughout the county. In the ninth century King Alfred fought against the Danes and was responsible for the defences still visible around his burh of Wareham. In 978 King Edward the

Martyr was murdered at Corfe. His body was later taken to Shaftesbury Abbey, where Cnut died in 1035. Seven years later, it was at Gillingham that the Witan proclaimed Edward the Confessor as king of England.

The Saxons have left only a little physical evidence, in churches and the Wareham defences. However, the Norman presence is most strongly seen in church architecture, from the tiny but perfect Studland to the great Christchurch Priory. The Dorset churches are an intimate part of the landscape. Many are old, but examples of the eighteenth and nineteenth centuries are of interest too, as are the villages in which they are found. Dorset has several medieval castles, including the romantic ruins of Corfe Castle, one of the best known in England. The monastic system had a strong influence in the middle ages, with establishments including Abbotsbury, Bindon, Cerne Abbas, Christchurch, Forde (then in Devon), Milton, Shaftesbury and Sherborne. Even Glastonbury Abbey (Somerset) had properties in Dorset. All this ended with the Dissolution in 1539. Except where the abbey church was transferred to the parish, the ruination of these great religious houses is now all but complete.

The seventeenth century saw dramatic

events in Dorset, and few key places had no share in the sieges and skirmishes of the Civil War. The Dorset Clubmen, formed to defend the county from the excesses of both parties, were routed by Cromwell at Hambledon Hill. Dorset is also associated with the escape of Charles II after the battle of Worcester in 1651. His adventures before he could take ship to the continent are well documented, from Trent in the north to Charmouth and Bridport in the south. The story of the ill-fated Monmouth Rebellion of 1685, which began at Lyme Regis, did not end at the battle of Sedgemoor. The aftermath left a trail of revenge administered by Judge Jeffreys; Monmouth was captured near Horton, east Dorset. Subsequent history has been more peaceful, although there was a threat of invasion during the Napoleonic Wars. In the 1860s defences were erected against the French around Portland Harbour and its breakwater. Portland has remained a naval base ever since. The army returned to Dorset in the twentieth century, with the establishment of the Royal Signals at Blandford Camp, and tank and gunnery ranges on the heaths at Bovington and Lulworth.

The rural scene of late nineteenth-century Dorset greatly influenced two local writers. Thomas Hardy (1840-1928) is world famous for the poems and novels of his 'Wessex', and places associated with these are considered in chapter 9. William Barnes (1801-86) is less widely known. This learned man of lowly origins was brought up in Sturminster Newton and ended his days as rector at Winterborne Came and Whitcombe, south of Dorchester. He is remembered for his poems written in the Dorset dialect.

Dorset today is still mainly rural. There are few towns in the interior, where agriculture is the main occupation and hamlets and villages are the norm. The largest settlement is Dorchester, the county town, which has a population of only fourteen thousand. It is a major route centre and to a lesser extent so is Blandford Forum. Other towns are Beaminster, Gillingham, Shaftesbury, Sherborne, Sturminster Newton and Wimborne Minster, all of which are good touring centres.

The south coast area is the busiest part of Dorset, as the beautiful coastline and mild climate have attracted the largest towns and a thriving tourist industry. Camping and caravanning are popular forms of accommodation along the undeveloped parts of the coast. There are the smaller resorts of Lyme Regis and Swanage, but there are two major centres. Weymouth was made famous as a resort by George III. It has a fine beach and is a ferry port for Cherbourg and the Channel Islands. The resort is deservedly popular, but it is far outstripped in size by the huge Poole-Bourne-mouth-Christchurch conurbation. This almost continuous urban area stretches for 12 miles (19 km) from west to east and is quite out of character with anywhere else in Dorset. Before 1974, when the county boundaries were adjusted, Bournemouth and Christchurch belonged to Hampshire. Poole had grown up since medieval times on a peninsula on the northern shore of its magnificent natural harbour. Christchurch, too, was important at that time, with its castle and priory, sited on a smaller harbour at the mouths of the rivers Avon and Stour. The growth of Bournemouth and its suburbs dates from the nineteenth century onwards and was closely associated with tourism. Its pleasant climate and position on the south coast have made it a desirable place for holidays or retirement.

Dorset has had few railways. The Somerset and Dorset Railway (1863-1965), which followed the Stour, is now but a trace across the valley floor. Branches to the south coast resorts of Bridport (West Bay), Lyme Regis and Swanage were also axed in the Beeching era. With the exception of the main Waterloo to Exeter line, which crosses the northern tip of the county, and a branch from Yeovil to Dorchester, the principal railway is in the south, serving Bournemouth and Weymouth. In the south, too, are the main industries. While fishing fleets are based at most harbours along the coast, some industries have a peculiarly Dorset flavour, such as the quarrying of stone at Portland, and stone and clay in Purbeck. Among the towns, Bridport is famous for its rope and net making. Poole is the county's major port, which takes advantage of the prolonged high tides experienced in the harbour. Coal, oil and other commodities are imported and there is a growing commercial vehicle ferry service to France. The power station at Hamworthy has shut down but is a prominent landmark. Poole Pottery developed from local sources of clay, and light industry is now important in the town. On Winfrith Heath, the Atomic Energy Authority's reactor contrasts with the landscape around. Oil has been extracted at Kimmeridge since about 1960, but a rich well was struck at Wytch Farm near Wareham in 1974. With the discovery of Britain's largest onshore reserve beneath Poole Harbour, there has been extensive surveying in the county, with exploration wells drilled as far north as the Blackmoor Vale.

THE CHALKLANDS

A broad band of chalk enters the county in the north-east and traverses central Dorset to within 5 miles (8 km) of Bridport in the west. One of the best ways to get the feel of the county is to follow the A354 from Salisbury to Blandford Forum and Puddletown, and thence westwards by the A35 through Dorchester to

A quiet corner of Powerstock, west Dorset.

Bridport. In the north-east, Cranborne Chase is an area of mainly arable farmland, rich in archaeology. There are few villages beside the A354 as it traverses the Chase before descending to Blandford Forum. Here, the river Stour meanders in a long corridor through the chalk. To the north-east of the town, the valley at Shillingstone is almost gorge-like where the river has cut through the high chalk escarpment on the edge of the Blackmoor Vale.

Between Blandford Forum and Dorchester the slopes steepen and there is more woodland. This is the heart of the chalk country, with high plateau land dissected by long, deep valleys, sometimes dry or with south-flowing streams such as the Cerne, Piddle and Winterborne. The last is the smallest, with a string of shrunken villages of medieval origin, but all are delightful to follow, with villages as attractive as their names. To the north the hills become higher, ending in the great escarpment which drops dramatically into the Blackmoor Vale. Some roads follow the escarpment itself and there are fine viewpoints along its length, such as at Batcombe and Bulbarrow. At the head of each of the chalk valleys there is often a gap or low col through which the valley road passes to gain the Vale below. The lane between Plush and Hazelbury Bryan passes through an imposing gap, flanked by Ball Hill and Nettlecombe Tout and visible from many miles away. Nearby is Lyscombe Bottom, a huge natural amphitheatre which must be seen to be believed. The road between Piddletrenthide and Cerne Abbas provides one of the best vistas of this high chalkland, with a mixture of pasture, arable and woodland.

To the west and north-west of Dorchester the chalk is further dissected. The main roads, after following the valleys, eventually emerge on the high chalk ridges, with exhilarating views. There is a mass of radio masts on Rampisham Hill, from where the BBC Overseas Service transmits in thirty-four languages. The valleys of the Bride, Frome, Sydling Water and their tributaries are well worth exploring for their beauty and inviting hamlets and villages.

South of Dorchester, an arm of the chalk swings eastwards and narrows to a steep-sided ridge. This is most prominent between Dorchester and Weymouth, where the railway is forced into a tunnel. High chalk cliffs traverse the coast on either side of Lulworth Cove, before taking the form of the Purbeck Hills, which end in the sea again at Old Harry Rocks. This long barrier across Purbeck is broken only once, at Corfe Castle.

THE HEATHLANDS

The horseshoe shape of the chalk district encloses the Tertiary clays and sands of the south-east Dorset part of the Hampshire Basin. In the west, they reach almost to Dorchester and form the 'Egdon Heath' loved by Thomas Hardy. Where the rivers Frome and Piddle cross the heathlands, they have formed fertile vales through the more barren ground on either side. In many places, such as around Puddletown and Wareham, the heaths have been planted with conifers. Forestry Commission walks here combine both forest and heath. Elsewhere the heath has fared less well. For example, it is used as a tank-driving ground outside Bovington Camp. To the south of the Frome, a large area of Winfrith Heath is taken up by the Atomic Energy Authority's research facilities and prototype steam-generating heavy water reactor, now mostly screened with trees.

The heaths are extensive on the south side of Poole Harbour, from the Arne peninsula to Studland, where there is an important nature reserve with rare flora and fauna. The Agglestone is a curious block of sloping and partly overhanging sandstone on the heath near Studland village. The heaths closer to the Purbeck Hills have long been under pressure, first from clay mining and quarrying, then from the army range on Povington Heath. The discovery of the large oilfield beneath the heaths and Poole Harbour has led to conflict over the means of extracting the oil. However, the Wytch Farm development is unobtrusive, with its 'nodding donkeys' pumping out the oil.

Between Poole and Wimborne Minister, Canford Heath is being steadily swallowed up by new housing developments. Northwards, the dormitory towns of Ferndown and West Moors have already taken heathland. The Holt and Horton heaths give way to indifferent farmland and woodland, more typical of the Hampshire Basin and fringes of the New Forest.

THE VALES

In contrast to the open spaces of the chalk downs and heathlands, the Dorset vales with their small fields and scattered woods convey a more peaceful feeling — almost of security. The large Blackmoor Vale lies to the north of the chalk escarpment, and its clay soils make it an important dairy farming area. Its attraction lies in its small fields with wooded hedgerows, and its dispersed villages. It was part of the old royal Blackmoor Forest, and the earthworks of a royal hunting lodge can be seen outside Gillingham in the north. Near King's Stag there is a large herd of fallow deer in the park of Stock Gaylard House.

The vale is drained by the Stour and its tributaries, leaving through the gap at Shillingstone. Hambledon Hill marks this exit and is dominant from many parts of the vale. In the north-east, the vale is overlooked by Shaftesbury, standing on a high spur of greensand. The dark, wooded Duncliffe Hill is an outlier and prominent feature in the vicinity. The floor of the vale is undulating, the lower land close to the Stour often flooding after heavy winter rain. The villages are on higher ground, such as Marnhull, a large settlement with some interesting buildings but no identifiable centre. Stalbridge suffers from a busy main road, but the quieter villages of Okeford Fitzpaine, Stour Provost and Stourton Caundle all have their charm. At remote Barnes Cross, not far from this last, is the oldest letter box in use in England (1853). The focus of the vale is at Sturminster Newton, with its medieval bridge

The quay at Wareham.

over the Stour. The important market serves most of the vale.

The Marshwood Vale, in the west of the county, is tiny. It is the vale of the river Char, flowing south-west to Charmouth, and is almost enclosed by high hills in the north and a range of coastal hills in the south. It is a vale of farms and the little village of Whitchurch Canonicorum is its only significant settlement. The trace of the so-called Marshwood Castle was a thirteenth-century moated house. In the north of the vale, Pilsdon Manor is now a retreat. At the east end, only a low hill at Broadoak separates the vale from the valley of the Simene, which flows to Bridport.

THE WEST DORSET HILLS

Between Lyme Regis and Sherborne, the erosion of Jurassic limestones and sands has created a land of intricate hills and valleys. Narrow lanes lead to farms and small hamlets. To the west of Bridport, the hills culminate in Golden Cap on the coast. To the east of the town, this partly wooded scenery continues north through Powerstock to Beaminster. The hills hereabouts rise to 908 feet (277 m) at Pilsdon Pen, the highest summit in Dorset. The landscape north of Sherborne lacks the individual hills but retains the steep wooded slopes and intricate valleys. On the Somerset border, an exploration of the lanes between Nether Compton and Poyntington is rewarding.

THE COAST

A traverse eastwards from Lyme Regis shows the great variety of the Dorset coast, most of it walkable by means of the Dorset Coast Path. The Black Ven lies between Lyme Regis and Charmouth and is noted for its landslips and fossils. East of the beach at Charmouth are the soft but impressive cliffs of Stonebarrow and Golden Cap, the highest point on the south coast of England. Seatown and Eype Mouth follow. From West Bay (Bridport's harbour) the vertical East Cliff, with its alternate layers of yellow sand and hard stone, leads to Burton Bradstock. The Chesil Beach now sweeps for 16 miles (25 km) towards Portland, a dramatic feature on any map. It leaves the mainland at Abbotsbury and its massive bank holds back a lagoon of brackish water — the Fleet. At the west end is the famous Abbotsbury Swannery. At the far end, the bank forms a causeway for the modern road from Weymouth to Fortuneswell on the Isle of Portland. The island itself points south and forms a conspicuous break in the general coastline.

East of Weymouth, past Osmington Mills, the cliffs are unstable. At Ringstead Bay is the Burning Cliff, where rapid oxidation of iron pyrites ignited the oil shales in 1826 and continued to smoke for about four years. Here begins the chalk, rising to White Nothe at the far end of the bay. In a section of cliff an unconformity can be observed, with the more horizontal chalk beds overlying steeply angled rocks. The chalk cliff top becomes steeply undulating where dry valleys meet the cliffs, when suddenly the natural limestone arch of Durdle Door is reached. This and Lulworth Cove are popular beauty spots. However, the crowds can be avoided by entering the army tank ranges (check when they are open) on the far side of the circular Lulworth Cove. The chalk cliffs of Worbarrow Bay, cut by the deep Arish Mell, present some of the most inspiring scenery of the whole coast. The jagged line of Mupe Rocks is the continuation of the vertical limestone seen at Durdle Door and Lulworth. It emerges from the sea again at Worbarrow Tout on the far side of the bay. The good beach here can be reached from the abandoned village of Tyneham, when the ranges are open. Behind the beach, reddish sands and clays are exposed in the low cliffs. The ranges have at least prevented the commercialisation of this lovely coast.

The alarming Gad Cliff follows, before the end of the ranges at Kimmeridge Bay, with its shales and oil well. The curious Chapman's Pool can be reached from Kingston or Worth Matravers, as can St Aldhelm's Head (also known as St Alban's Head), with its Norman chapel and coastguard station. This is high limestone country and well into the Isle of Purbeck region. There are very fine medieval strip lynchets below the village of Worth Matravers, in the valley leading down to Winspit. On the coast here and at Seacombe there are underground stone quarries. Dancing Ledge is popular, as it gives access to the sea along an otherwise inhospitable coast. This steep section to the lighthouse at Anvil Point is the realm of rock climbers and nesting sea birds. At Durlston Head, the cliffs form part of a country park. The coastline turns north from here, past the dangerous ledges off Peveril Point, to Swanage Bay.

The town of Swanage looks out towards the chalk Ballard Cliff, at the end of the Purbeck ridge last seen at Worbarrow Bay. At the Foreland, erosion by the sea has created tall chalk stacks, including the Old Harry Rocks. They point towards the Needles on the Isle of Wight, where the chalk re-appears. Studland is popular for its long sandy beach and dunes, uncommercialised and close to Bournemouth via the Sandbanks ferry. The Studland and Sandbanks peninsulas enclose Poole Harbour, which is a haven for yachtsmen. It is among the largest natural harbours in the world, though not deep. Much of the southern part contains mud flats and intricate creeks and islands of great interest. After Bournemouth

7

and its long, groyne-protected beaches, Hengistbury Head is the last landmark on the Dorset coast. It forms a high promontory of weak sandstones at the entrance to Christchurch Harbour. There is evidence for occupation here from palaeolithic times down to the iron age, when it was an important port. In the nineteenth century an attempt was made to quarry ironstone, but today its heathy summit is a popular place to walk.

ISLE OF PORTLAND

The southern tip of Dorset and an island but for Chesil Beach, Portland rises from sea level at the Bill to 480 feet (146 m) in the north, forming an easily recognised outline. There are fine views along the coast from the summit. Since the influence of Sir Christopher Wren in the seventeenth century, the quarrying of Portland stone has made the island famous but also destroyed much of its surface. Some quarries are still doing so, and, if not beautiful, the landscape is unique. Portland Bill is the 'Land's End' of Dorset. Apart from the lighthouse, there is evidence of small quarries along the coast and old strip fields still in use, and offshore a terrific tide race. Convict labour was used when the first breakwater was built (1847-72) and large quarries were opened up for that purpose in the north of the island. The old stone-built prison became the borstal when it was moved to the Verne Citadel. At Castletown the naval base is used mainly by ships working up after refits or for training. The great breakwaters of Portland Harbour form a sheltered anchorage and there are frequent arrivals and sailings.

ISLE OF PURBECK

Not a true island but a distinct region south of Wareham and east of Lulworth Cove, Purbeck combines both inland and coastal scenery, where its great interest is due to the changing geology, aligned from west to east. In the north, and bordering Poole Harbour, are the heaths of the Tertiary sands and clays. There is woodland, too. Clay has been mined and quarried to the west of Corfe Castle, and narrow-gauge railways once took the clay to shipping places on the shores of Poole Harbour. The Blue Pool is the best known of the abandoned and flooded clay pits.

The long line of the chalk Purbeck Hills is broken at Corfe Castle. Wealden (Cretaceous) clays and sands form a broad sheltered vale to the south, from Tyneham to Swanage. This is a gentle area of farms, woodland and attractive stone settlements. Parallel with the south coast are more uplands — the hard Jurassic limestones of the Portland and Purbeck series. These include Purbeck marble, a freshwater shelly limestone which takes a good polish. It was worked by the Romans, and Corfe Castle became the centre of the industry in medieval times. More recently it was mined and traces of shafts can be seen behind Swanage. Apart from Wareham at the gateway to Purbeck, the only town is Swanage, a busy resort. More attractive are the picturesque villages of Purbeck, all in local stone, such as Church Knowle, Corfe Castle, Kimmeridge, Langton Matravers and Worth Matravers, and the churches, especially the Norman ones at Studland and Worth Matravers.

Wimborne Minster.

8

The Blue Pool.

2
The countryside

Avon Forest Park, 3 miles (5 km) east of Ferndown. Telephone: Ringwood (0425) 478082.

This comprises 580 acres (235 ha) of mixed heath and pine woods. There are picnic areas and woodland walks in the North and South Parks, while viewpoints at Matchams View look out over the Avon valley towards the New Forest.

Batcombe picnic site, near Minterne Magna.

On the road between Holywell and Dogbury Gate (Minterne Magna), this is a large area with picnic places at different levels on the edge of the partly wooded chalk escarpment. There are extensive views northwards over the Blackmoor Vale and distant Somerset.

Bishop's Limekiln picnic site, Abbotsbury.

A tiny site beside the steep lane between Abbotsbury and the Hardy Monument, it features a partly restored limekiln and good views southwards towards the coast.

The Blue Pool, Furzebrook, near Wareham. Telephone: Wareham (0929) 551408.

This well known beauty spot is a flooded nineteenth-century clay pit. It earns its name from the minute clay particles in suspension in the water, changing its colour from deep blue to green according to the amount of sunlight. It was opened to the public in 1935 and is surrounded by pine woods through which there are walks with glimpses of the pool. There are shops, a teahouse and a small museum.

Brownsea Island, Poole Harbour. National Trust. Telephone: Canford Cliffs (0202) 707744.

Approached by ferries from Poole Quay and Sandbanks, Brownsea at 500 acres (202 ha) is the largest of the five islands in Poole Harbour, and it gives fine views all round, notably towards the harbour entrance and Purbeck. There is much variety here, including woodlands, heath and grassland. Wildlife includes red squirrels, extinct on the surrounding mainland, and shy sika deer, introduced in 1896. There are also many peacocks.

The northern half is a nature reserve (Dorset Trust for Nature Conservation), with a large lagoon, lakes and an important heronry among the trees. At the east end of the island is the landing stage and a small settlement of crenellated cottages. Some of these were once part of a coastguard station. The castle (chapter 4) is not open to the public. The church (St Mary) was built in 1854 and contains a fifteenth-century timber roof from Crosby Palace, Bishopsgate, London, and various treasures added by subsequent owners of the island.

The then owner, Colonel Waugh, was responsible for much development in the mid nineteenth century, such as the twin-towered family landing pier, later additions to the castle and a modern farm. He also developed a pottery industry at the west end of the island. This was never a great success and closed in 1887. Fragments of the sewage pipes and sanitary wares made here are strewn along the shore, while the workers' village of Maryland lies ruined beneath the trees. In the early twentieth century an attempt was made to grow daffodils for Covent Garden, and their descendants can be seen in the meadows in the south-east. Baden-Powell held his first experimental camp of twenty boys on the island in 1907. A stone commemorates this event, which led to the formation of the Scouting movement. Below is an area allocated for camping by scouts and guides. In 1934 two-thirds of the island was ravaged by fire. This danger is ever present and the thousands of annual visitors are reminded to be careful.

Bulbarrow and Ibberton Hill picnic site

The site is just east of the true Bulbarrow Hill, 5 miles (8 km) south of Sturminster Newton. This is one of Dorset's great viewpoints, looking out over the Blackmoor Vale to the distant hills of the Blackdowns, Quantocks and Mendips. There is a good picnic site at Ibberton Hill, a little lower to the north-east.

Chesil Beach

The Isle of Portland is joined to the mainland by this 10 mile (16 km) bank of shingle. Access is easiest at Fortuneswell, Portland, or at Abbotsbury, where a lane leads down to the bank. Between these points is the enclosed semi-tidal and brackish water of the Fleet. The beach continues westwards along the coast for another 7 miles (11 km) until it is broken by the harbour entrance at West Bay. Walking along it is hard going. The larger flint pebbles found at the Portland end have been gradually reduced to finer material at Abbotsbury and West Bay. This is the result of longshore drift, which works here in the reverse direction to that normally experienced on the south coast. It is said that local fishermen, landing in a fog or at night, can tell where they are on the beach by the size of the pebbles. A series of stepped storm beaches features throughout the length of Chesil Beach. Despite its apparent great height, severe storms have breached it, such as in February 1979, when Fortuneswell was badly flooded.

Dorset Coast Path

This the best way to discover the variety and splendour of Dorset's coastline. The long-distance path is waymarked for 72 miles (116 km) from Lyme Regis to Poole Harbour. It was officially opened in 1974 as Dorset's contribution to the much longer South-West Peninsula Coast Path. The only disappointing section is around Weymouth, but an alternative route strikes inland between West Bexington and Osmington Mills. This follows the South Dorset Ridgeway for some distance, which makes a good contrast to the coastal scenery. For a summary of the coast, see chapter 1.

Durdle Door, West Lulworth.

Approach by the coast path from Lulworth Cove or from Daggers Gate. A huge archway of Portland stone lurches into the sea like a great beast's head. Earth movements have folded the rock strata into a near vertical position, parallel with the present coastline, and the T-shaped promontory is a result of differential erosion. It is separated from the chalk mainland by a narrow neck of weak sands. The Man o' War Rocks jut into the blue waters of St Oswald's Bay on the Lulworth side. There are good shingle beaches on both sides of the headland.

Durlston Country Park, Swanage. Telephone: Swanage (0929) 424443.

There are an information centre and toilets at the car park, 1 mile (1.6 km) south of Swanage. This 261 acre (105 ha) coastal park includes George Burt's nineteenth-century Durlston Castle at Durlston Head. Here also is his Great Globe of 1887. It weighs 40 tons and is made of fifteen segments of Portland stone, carved with the continents of the worlds. The cliff path gives views of the Tillywhim Caves, with stones inscribed with verses. The 'caves', former quarries, are no longer open to the public because of their dangerous condition. A capstan has been restored at the entrance to an underground stone quarry, next to the road to the lighthouse at Anvil Point. The white pylons erected on the coast mark the 'measured mile' used by ships on speed trials. The cliffs below and to the west of the lighthouse are very steep and are an important rock-climbing area.

Fontmell and Melbury Downs, near Shaftesbury. National Trust.

There is a small car park here, 3 miles (5 km) south-east of Shaftesbury and close to Compton Abbas airfield. There are fine views westwards over the Blackmoor Vale, complementing the views from nearby Win Green (Wiltshire). Below, the fifteenth-century tow-

Stair Hole and Lulworth Cove.

er is all that remains of the church at West Compton, now surrounded by farm buildings. There is a nature reserve in an area of unimproved chalk downland. Archaeological remains include traces of field systems and a very fine example of a crossdyke, cutting across the neck of the spur. It is a good walk across Compton Down to Melbury Beacon, the distinctive highest point just to the north.

Golden Cap, near Chideock. National Trust.
This is the crowning glory of a large clifftop estate of great attraction, between Charmouth and West Bay. It is the highest point on the south coast of England, at 626 feet (191 m), and makes a fine viewpoint. Its distinctive plateau top is capped with golden sandstone, seen to advantage from a distance, such as from the Cobb at Lyme Regis. Golden Cap can be approached by the steep coast path from Seatown (east) or, less strenuously, from near Morcombelake (inland).

Hardy Monument, Black Down, near Dorchester. National Trust.
This is a prominent landmark from many miles away, on the summit of Black Down, 5 miles (8 km) south-west of Dorchester. It is a broad-based octagonal tower of stone, erected in 1844 to the memory of Admiral Sir Thomas Masterman Hardy, who was Nelson's flag captain at Trafalgar. His former house is below, in Portesham village. Close to, the tower is not very attractive, and the hilltop is scruffy with gorse and gravel. However, at 777 feet (237 m), it is a magnificent viewpoint,

south to the English Channel and north across much of Dorset. There are many bronze age round barrows in the vicinity.

Kimmeridge Bay, Purbeck.
There is hardly a beach here, but instead there are extensive flat ledges of dark Kimmeridge shales. These rocks are known for their fossils and oil content — when freshly broken, there is a distinct aroma. The shale has been carved into ornaments since the bronze age. More recently, there were attempts at working it for its fuel content, and there are traces of tramways and tunnels along the cliffs. The 'nodding donkey' of an oil well pumps small quantities from a reservoir at a greater depth. Output is measured in a few lorry loads per week. On the headland above the tiny quay is Clavel's Tower, a nineteenth-century watchtower. Sir William Clavell built Smedmore House (chapter 5). Kimmeridge village is small but pretty. It lies a short distance inland but must be passed to reach the bay.

Lulworth Cove, West Lulworth.
This much visited cove is almost a complete circle where the sea has broken through an outer barrier of hard limestone to erode the softer clays and sands behind. It is backed by the steep chalk cliffs of Bindon Hill. In summer the car park is huge and almost dwarfs the small community with its souvenir and tea shops. The cove provides a sheltered anchorage, and some fishing boats work from here. Stair Hole is an attraction, where the sea is

forcing its way through steeply dipping and folded rocks. Across the cove is the Fossil Forest. This is exposed on sloping limestone beds and is designated as a geological reserve. Nearby was the first Bindon Abbey, before the Cistercians moved to their final inland site near Wool in 1172. To the west, the coast path leads to Durdle Door.

Pilsdon Pen, near Broadwindsor. National Trust.

This is the highest point in Dorset, at 908 feet (277 m). The B3164 from Broadwindsor passes below and there is a small lay-by. There are extensive views from the hilltop: south over the Marshwood Vale to the coast, and westwards to Dartmoor in Devon. An iron age hillfort defends the southern end of this long hill (chapter 3).

Portland Bill, Isle of Portland.

This is the lowest and most southern point of Portland and Dorset, almost at sea level. Offshore is the fierce Portland tide race. The tall red and white lighthouse dates from 1905, and its two predecessors can be seen a little inland. Just west of the point is the Pulpit Rock. Nearby, the remnants of a 'raised beach' were formed when sea level was higher. There are disused quarries along the low cliffs, where derrick cranes are now used to haul small boats in and out of the sea. Here also are survivals of the old strip fields ('lawnsheds'), once common over much of the island. The observatory in an old lighthouse is a reminder that Portland is one of the stepping-off or landing points for migrant birds.

Portland Heights viewpoint, Isle of Portland.

At the top of the island, beside the Portland Heights Hotel and reached by a steep climb from Fortuneswell, a car park provides a viewpoint and a base to explore the old quarries at this end of the island. On most days, the sweep of Chesil Beach below is impressive as it recedes towards West Bay, but on the clearest days the coast can be followed to Start Point in south Devon. The hills of Dartmoor are also visible. This is among the finest coastal views in England.

Stanpit Marsh Nature Reserve, Christchurch.

This is an area of marshland which juts into Christchurch Harbour, making a notable viewpoint for estuarine birds.

Studland Bay and Old Harry Rocks, Purbeck. National Trust.

Popular sandy beaches stretch around Studland Bay northwards for 3 miles (5 km) to Shell Bay and the entrance to Poole Harbour.

Much is backed by low dunes, but there are low cliffs at the south end, below Studland village. High chalk cliffs to the east terminate in the sea stacks known as Old Harry Rocks, at the Foreland or Handfast Point. There are dramatic cliffs between here and Ballard Point, with further superb chalk stacks — the Pinnacle and Haystack. There are caves and arches at sea level. All this was given to the National Trust in 1981.

Studland Heath Nature Reserve, Studland, Purbeck.

An important heathland and wetland area between low coastal sand dunes and the southern shore of Poole Harbour, this site includes birch woods, reed beds and a freshwater lake known as the Little Sea. The great range of plants includes the early marsh orchid and rare Dorset heath, while the sand lizard and smooth snake are rare examples of wildlife. A nature trail is laid out in the summer.

Thorncombe Wood, Higher Bockhampton.

This is a fine area of mixed woodland close to Thomas Hardy's Cottage (chapter 9) at Higher Bockhampton, 3 miles (5 km) east of Dorchester. There are information boards at the car park, where nature trail leaflets are available. A delightful walk leads through mature deciduous woods to Hardy's Cottage, while longer walks lead to remnants of the heath. Traces of the Roman road from Dorchester to Badbury Rings can be detected just south of the car park.

Tyneham village, Purbeck.

This now derelict village and its whole valley were taken over for military training during the Second World War. They still remain within the army's tank ranges. However, there is public access when there is no firing. The roofless houses still give an impression of the layout of the village, and the restored church, with its small exhibition, is worth a visit. There is a large parking area, from which the track leads past targets to the fine beach at Worbarrow Bay. Ruined houses tell of a fishing community.

Winyard's Gap and Crook Hill, Corscombe. National Trust.

Near the Somerset border, beside the A356 about 4 miles (6 km) south-east of Crewkerne, there are 16 acres (6.5 ha) of woodland, given to the National Trust as a memorial to the men of the 43rd (Wessex) Division who fell in the Second World War. Crook Hill, on the end of a spur just to the north-east, gives good views across this part of the county and Somerset beyond.

12

Maiden Castle, near Dorchester.

3
Archaeological sites

Dorset ranks among the richest archaeological counties in England, with representative examples of many types of field monuments. A glance at an Ordnance Survey map will reveal the density of prehistoric and Roman sites, mostly confined to the more amenable chalklands, with less evidence on the sandy heaths of the south-east. Cranborne Chase was the scene of excavations by General Pitt-Rivers in the late nineteenth century. These were of a high standard and earned him a name as the father of modern archaeology. Among his excavations was the Wor Barrow, a neolithic long barrow.

The earliest evidence for man's presence in Dorset is an occasional palaeolithic hand-axe of flint, recovered from river gravels. They may possibly date back to eighty thousand years ago. There is more evidence from finds of mesolithic flints, notably from Hengistbury Head and Portland. A stone shelter of about 5200 BC has been excavated at Culver Well, south Portland. However, there is nothing to see on the ground until the neolithic period, about 3500 BC, when the history of man in Dorset becomes expressed in an abundance of monuments.

The neolithic people were the first agriculturalists, with time to spare for the construction of ritual monuments. The earliest were collective tombs known as long barrows, some with stone chambers. Much longer bank barrows have been identified in the south of the county. Earlier neolithic ritual centres include the causewayed enclosures at Hambledon Hill and Maiden Castle. Traces of the former are recognisable, but the latter lies beneath an iron age hillfort. Mount Pleasant at Dorchester was the largest of the late neolithic henges, enclosing 11 acres (4.5 ha). It was partially excavated in 1970-1, to reveal a ditch surrounding the post holes for a huge circular timber structure, probably a building similar to that at Woodhenge in Wiltshire. Another henge, as large as Mount Pleasant, was discovered in Dorchester in 1984. Knowlton is the site of three henges in a row, although only one is well preserved. Possibly the most important neolithic site is the Dorset Cursus, over 6 miles (9.6 km) in length and still a mystery. The ploughed-out trace of at least one lesser cursus has been revealed by aerial photography to the west of Dorchester.

Cemeteries of round barrows (tumuli) are the principal monuments of the bronze age. There are hundreds of barrows, mainly of the early bronze age, often in fine locations. While most are on the chalklands, there are some on the heaths, such as at Povington. Some have yielded rich grave goods, including gold, amber and shale. Kimmeridge was the source of shale beads, bracelets and cups, which have also been found outside the county, indicating trade. A few ritual stone circles survive in south Dorset, reflecting the availability of suitable stone there. The most accessible is the small Nine Stones. Settlements and field systems are difficult to identify, but a small middle bronze age farm was excavated at Shearplace Hill near Sydling St Nicholas.

Iron age fields — rectangular earthworks, often called 'Celtic fields' — abound on the unploughed chalk pastureland of central Dorset. They are best seen in the winter, when the sun casts long shadows from the low banks, or lynchets. It is likely that many of these fields remained in use in Romano-British times. Farming settlements also continued to be occupied by the local inhabitants and may survive as low earthworks which are difficult to interpret on the ground. At Woodcutts, Cranborne Chase, Pitt-Rivers restored the earthworks to give some idea of the layout. An excavated site at Gussage All Saints produced evidence for metalworking.

Dorset has some of the finest iron age hillforts in England, including Badbury Rings, Eggardon Hill, Hambledon Hill, Hod Hill and Maiden Castle. Such monuments reflect both the development of regional centres and the greater need for defence, as growing pressures for land led to conflict between tribal groups. Dorset was the territory of the Durotriges. In the late iron age Hengistbury Head was their main port, trading with the continent and the Roman world. Evidence for seafaring includes an iron anchor and chain, dating from the first century AD. This was found at Bulbury Camp in 1881 and, being so far inland, it is believed to have been part of a smith's scrap iron collection.

Archaeology provides evidence for the passing of Vespasian's Second Legion through Dorset at the time of the Roman invasion of AD 43. The best known site is Maiden Castle. Here and at Spettisbury Rings war cemeteries have been found, while at Hod Hill the Romans built their own fort. Less well known early Roman forts have been investigated at Lake, near Wimborne and Waddon Hill, Stoke Abbott. Finds from the latter are displayed in Bridport Museum. An earthwork at Winterbourne Steepleton is believed to have been a signal station.

The Roman town of Dorchester (*Durnovaria*) was established a short distance from Maiden Castle. Important finds have been made over the years and can be seen in the County Museum (chapter 7). The town walls and an aqueduct can be traced, there is a town house displayed at Colliton, and the amphitheatre is at Maumbury Rings. Ports were established at Hamworthy (Poole) and Radipole (Weymouth). Roads converged on Dorchester and Badbury Rings, and these are often followed by modern roads. The best preserved section of a Roman road is the Ackling Dyke, Cranborne Chase. There is little or nothing to see of villa sites, but a mosaic from the one at Hinton St Mary is in the British Museum. At its centre is the chi-rho symbol behind what may be an early representation of Christ's head, although it could also be Constantine the Great, who legalised Chrisianity in the Roman world. The Christian chi-rho symbol was inscribed on two silver rings found in a hoard at the nearby Fifehead Neville villa. While there is evidence for Christianity here, pagan religion is seen in the Cerne Abbas Giant and the temples at Jordan Hill and Maiden Castle. Roman industries included the working of Kimmeridge shale (there are carved table legs in the County Museum) and Purbeck marble.

The late Roman and post-Roman periods were troubled times, reflected in the construction of Bokerley Dyke on Cranborne Chase. There is a lack of dark age monuments, although the hillfort at Badbury Rings is one of several contenders for the site of Arthur's Battle of Mount Badon at the beginning of the sixth century. The Saxon tide was stemmed for a generation and then continued apace. The earthworks around Wareham mark the defences of King Alfred's burh of the late ninth century and are the principal monument of the Saxon period in Dorset.

Later earthworks which are common in the Dorset landscape are strip lynchets. These are terraces constructed in medieval times to allow the cultivation of steep slopes. There are very fine examples at Worth Matravers, which are among the best in England. Others can be seen at the Bride Valley and beside the A35, east of Bridport.

The continuing danger to archaeological sites from agriculture and other causes is made plain in the new exhibition gallery at the County Museum in Dorchester. Finds from excavations are displayed here and at most local museums.

In the following gazetteer of sites, the six-figure National Grid reference for each site is preceded by the number of the Ordnance Survey 1:50,000 map on which it may be located.

NEOLITHIC

Dorset Cursus, Cranborne Chase (OS 184, 195; ST 969125 to SU 040192).

The longest example of its type in England, the Cursus stretches in two adjoined sections for 6¼ miles (10 km), south-west to north-east and almost parallel with the A354. The cursus has two parallel banks with outer ditches, about 100 yards (91 m) apart. Much has been ploughed out, but the high bank of the south-west terminus is seen next to a minor road on Thickthorn Down. The best preserved section of one bank and ditch crosses the B3081 at SU 018159 (not to be confused with the Roman road nearby). The north-east terminus has associated long barrows, which can be approached on foot from Woodyates or

Bokerley Dyke. For such a large monument, surprisingly little is known of its purpose.

Grey Mare and her Colts, near Abbotsbury (OS 194; SY 584871).

The best of the small group of chambered tombs in south Dorset, this is approached by a road and bridleway from Abbotsbury. It is sited on a gentle slope at the head of a valley. The stones of the chamber and forecourt survive at the eastern end, as does part of the kerb. The design is similar to a group of tombs mostly found in southern Scotland.

Hambledon Hill causewayed enclosure (OS 194; SY 848123).

Only the southern part of this monument, best approached by the bridleway from Child Okeford, has been spared from ploughing. The enclosure encircles the summit of the strangely shaped hill better known for its hillfort. Such an enclosure is identified by the discontinuous ditch surrounding an inner earthwork. Important excavations in 1974-80 revealed this to have been a mortuary site, with skulls placed in the surrounding ditches. Within, ritual offerings were placed in pits and the dead were exposed in the open air until their bones could be selected and taken to nearby long barrows (an example can be seen inside the hillfort). This ritual centre and its associated earthworks have been dated to about 3500 BC. On the Stepleton spur of the

hill an enclosed settlement was found — the first of its type in Britain. There was evidence that it had been attacked and overrun. Its economy appears to have been based on dairying at one stage.

The Hellstone, Portesham (OS 194; SY 605867).

Just north of Portesham, this low chambered tomb was incorrectly restored in 1866.

Knowlton Circles, near Wimborne St Giles (OS 195; SU 024103). English Heritage.

Close to the B3078 Cranborne to Wimborne road, there were once three circles in a row, of which the central one is the best preserved. This henge has a bank with an internal ditch, about 320 feet (97 m) in diameter. The site is enhanced by the ruined church of twelfth-century origin, showing the continuity of a religious site. A large tree-covered barrow is conspicuous just to the east. The larger south circle can be traced with difficulty as it crosses the field on the far side of the road junction.

Martin's Down bank barrow, Long Bredy (OS 194; SY 572912).

Extra-long types of barrow are mainly confined to this part of Dorset. This example is 645 feet (196 m) long and 6 feet (2 m) high and stands out clear on the crest of Martin's Down. Access is restricted, but it is easily seen from the A35 to the west.

The Grey Mare and her Colts is a chambered tomb near Abbotsbury.

Pimperne long barrow, Pimperne, near Blandford Forum (OS 195; ST 917105).

Easily passed, but close to the A354, opposite the turning to Blandford Camp, this is one of the finest examples of an earthen long barrow, 350 feet (107 m) long and about 9 feet (3 m) high. There are side ditches, separated by a berm. The barrow is aligned towards the south-south-east, but the more usual easterly alignment is seen at the nearby Thickthorn Bar long barrow (ST 951128), which is 320 feet (97 m) long and approached by a bridleway just south of Chettle.

BRONZE AGE
Clandon Barrow, Winterbourne St Martin (OS 194; SY 655890).

This large early bronze age round barrow can be seen on a hillside, to the east of Martinstown and west of Maiden Castle. It contained a rich grave of a Wessex culture leader. A lozenge-shaped gold plate from here is comparable with one from the famous Bush Barrow, near Stonehenge. Gold studs decorating a shale macehead, an amber cup and a bronze dagger are among the other grave goods.

Deverel Barrow, Milborne St Andrew (OS 194; SY 820990).

When this barrow was opened in 1824 by W. A. Miles, he found a semicircle of sarsen stones and a number of cists, containing seventeen cremations in bucket and globular urns. The site is important to archaeologists as

it gave its name to the Deverel-Rimbury style of bronze age pottery. It is marked by a partly broken-down flint wall with trees and the sarsen stones inside. A footpath crossing fields from the A354 passes the barrow.

Hampton Down stone circle, Portesham (OS 194; SY 596864).

This circle is a puzzle. It is only 35 feet (11 m) in diameter and is possibly the remains of the kerb of a round barrow, since disturbed.

Kingston Russell stone circle (OS 194; SY 577878). English Heritage.

On a plateau top, visible from and within walking distance of the Grey Mare and her Colts, this is a small circle, with a diameter of about 80 feet (25 m). All eighteen stones lie fallen and are difficult to see during the summer when the vegetation is high.

Nine Barrow Down barrow cemetery, Ailwood, near Swanage (OS 195; SY 996815).

This well known barrow group is sited atop the spectacular ridge of the Purbeck Hills. There is also a long barrow here. The barrows look down on the Rempstone circle.

Nine Stones stone circle, Winterbourne Abbas (OS 194; 611904). English Heritage.

Beneath trees on the south side of the A35, where it is easily missed and difficult to stop, this is a tiny circle of nine standing stones, about 25 feet (8 m) in diameter, unusual for its valley-floor setting.

The ruined church at Knowlton Circles.

Bronze age round barrows on Oakley Down.

Oakley Down barrow cemetery, Cranborne Chase (OS 184; SU 018173).

This famous barrow group lies in an area rich in archaeology, beside the A354 and cut by the Ackling Dyke Roman road. One large bell barrow is conspicuous and there are at least four disc barrows, with two or three low mounds within. Sir Richard Colt Hoare excavated here in the early nineteenth century and found cremations with amber beads in the disc barrows.There are many other barrows in the vicinity, some ploughed out, while across the road can be seen the Wor Barrow, the long barrow excavated by Pitt-Rivers in 1893-4.

Poor Lot barrow cemetery, Kingston Russell (OS 194; SY 587907). English Heritage.

On both sides of the A35, 6 miles (10 km) west of Dorchester, the cemetery is noted for its variety of barrow types, including a possible triple barrow and a twinned bell barrow. Much of this once very fine barrow group has been destroyed by ploughing since the Second World War.

Rempstone stone circle, Purbeck (OS 195; SY 995821).

Among trees, beside the B3351 road from Corfe Castle to Studland, this is an easterly outlier of the south Dorset stone circles. Only a few stones remain standing, and part of the circle has been damaged by the cutting of a trench across the site. Possible traces of an associated stone avenue to the west have been discovered by ploughing.

South Dorset Ridgeway barrows (OS 194; SY 613876 to SY 794842).

The high east-west ridge which separates Dorchester from Weymouth is the location for many round barrow groups, at times almost continuous. Many are prominent on the skyline from both sides, such as along Bronkham

Hill, just east of the Hardy Monument. Above Sutton Poyntz, a line of at least nine barrows is clearly visible from the coast. Towards the east, the ridge becomes less distinct. The Five Marys barrows are well sited on the last, very narrow ridge near Chaldon Herring. There are actually more than five barrows here, and nineteenth-century excavations found bodies with antlers on their shoulders. Other barrows are scattered on Chaldon Down, nearer the coast.

IRON AGE

Abbotsbury Castle, Abbotsbury (OS 194; SY 555865).

This univallate hillfort at the west end of the South Dorset Ridgeway forms a fine viewpoint, overlooking the sea and the Bride valley. Hut platforms can be seen within.

Badbury Rings, near Wimborne (OS 195; ST 965030). National Trust.

A large multivallate hillfort, with three ramparts and a tree-covered interior of 17 acres (7 ha), Badbury Rings has been cleared of scrub and the earthworks have been conserved, but it has never been excavated. Roman roads from Old Sarum, Bath, Dorchester and Poole meet here. The fort is among the possible sites of Mons Badonicus (Mount Badon), at which Arthur is reputed to have won a decisive victory over the Saxons. Point-to-point races are held on the downs in front of the fort, which lies close to the B3082 from Wimborne Minster to Blandford Forum.

Buzbury Rings, Tarrant Keynston (OS 195; ST 918060).

On Keynston Down and bisected by the B3082 road, from which they are visible, the grassy earthworks are smoothed on the east side of the road, where there is a golf course.

17

This was probably a defended settlement rather than a hillfort.

Eggardon Hill, Askerswell (OS 194; SY 540946). National Trust.

Spectacularly sited along a windswept spur, looking towards the Marshwood Vale, this great multivallate hillfort encloses 36 acres (14 ha). The defences are complex at the eastern end, which is the easiest approach. Traces of storage pits can be seen within. Just to the east, in West Compton parish, there are barrows, field systems and a few remaining stones of a burial chamber.

Flowers Barrow, East Lulworth (OS 194; SY 864805).

A coastal fort, within the army tank ranges, Flowers Barrow can be approached by a steep climb from both sides on the Dorset Coast Path. It was easily defended on the south side by the chalk cliffs of Worbarrow Bay, over which part of the fort has collapsed. The fort is at the west end of a narrow ridge. This is the easiest approach and it is defended by an outer crossdyke. Westwards, towards Lulworth Cove, the long, narrow ridge of Bindon Hill is the site of an iron age earthwork enclosing 400 acres (160 ha). This may have been the beach-head of an invasion, or it was built to protect a trading post.

Foretop, Fontmell Down (OS 183; ST 883183). National Trust.

Crossdykes are fairly common on the narrow necks of the chalk downs and are believed to be territorial boundaries. This example is well preserved and easily seen from the minor road from Melbury Abbas to Blandford Forum. It can be reached on foot from a small car park. There are field systems on Fontmell Down beyond.

Hambledon Hill, Child Okeford (OS 194; ST 845124).

This is one of the great hillforts of Dorset. Triple ramparts are seen contouring around the north-west spur of the hill, overlooking Child Okeford and Shroton villages. Hut platforms are clearly visible within. Note also the massive ramparts and ditches defending the east end. Like Maiden Castle, this fort shows signs of having been enlarged in the past. It is well sited, to control the narrow Stour valley at its exit from the Blackmoor Vale. The valley was almost certainly a trading route from Hengistbury Head on the coast, and this is also the crossing point of the Dorset Ridgeway.

Hengistbury Head, Christchurch Harbour (OS 195; SZ 175905).

Cut off by the housing estates of the Bournemouth conurbation, this long headland shelters Christchurch Harbour. It has been the scene of occupation on many occasions, from the palaeolithic onwards. In the iron age, its narrow neck was defended by a double bank and ditch. There was a busy trading port here in the century preceding the Roman conquest. Excavations have revealed evidence for metalworking, with a possible mint, and the importation of wine amphorae from the Roman world. The port lay at the mouth of the river Stour, which aided trade with the hinterland of the Durotriges as far upstream as Hod and Hambledon Hills, and beyond.

Hod Hill, Stourpaine (OS 194; ST 856105). National Trust.

Another great hillfort, enclosing 52 acres (21 ha), Hod Hill is next to Hambledon Hill, stressing the importance of the Stour valley at this point. Entrances with similar outworks are found at both forts, suggesting the same architect. On the west side of Hod Hill, the defences make use of the very steep slope eroded by the Stour. Elsewhere, large quarries behind the main rampart provided material for strengthening the defences before the Roman invasion. Depressions mark the sites of round huts. Excavations of one large hut and an enclosure showed evidence for a concentrated bombardment by a Roman ballista before the fort surrendered. The Romans built a fort in the north-west corner, where is found the steepest but shortest approach.

Maiden Castle, Dorchester (OS 194; SY 668884). English Heritage.

Maiden Castle, the most famous hillfort in southern England, from a distance appears insignificant on a low hill, belying the massive fortifications. Excavations by Sir Mortimer Wheeler in the 1930s showed the earliest fort to be on the site of a neolithic causewayed enclosure at the east end. It was then enlarged to enclose 47 acres (19 ha). Subsequent developments included huge multivallate defences and complex entrances, especially at the west end. The ramparts were defended by slingstones, and ammunition dumps of beach pebbles were provided at intervals. However, the Romans were able to storm the east entrance, where a hastily dug war cemetery may provide evidence for a massacre. Retaining drystone walls at the entrance were left exposed after excavation. Four thousand people may have lived at this important regional centre, but about thirty years after the conquest the population was removed to the new town of Dorchester. Activity returned in the fourth century, with the building of a Roman temple on the hill. The fort was the scene of further excavations in 1985-6.

Nettlecombe Tout, Higher Melcombe (OS 194; ST 736031).

This is a high, airy part of central Dorset, and footpaths approach from several directions. The promontory fort on Nettlecombe Tout may have never been completed, but it appears to be associated with a complex of crossdykes, fields and settlements around the huge amphitheatre of Lyscombe Bottom.

Pilsdon Pen, near Broadwindsor (OS 193; ST 412013). National Trust.

Close to the B3164, this elongated hillfort is at the south end of the highest hill in Dorset. It commands the Marshwood Vale and surrounding country far below. The excavation of some round huts provided evidence for goldworking and a Roman ballista bolt.

Poundbury Camp, Dorchester (OS 194; SY 682911).

On the north-west fringes of modern Dorchester, beside the river Frome, this small hillfort encloses 15 acres (6 ha). The Roman aqueduct to Dorchester follows the northern defences, and the railway from Yeovil (1857) plunges through a tunnel beneath the fort.

Rawlsbury Camp, Bulbarrow (OS 194; ST 767057).

This is a good example of a spur fort, near Bulbarrow and overlooking the Blackmoor Vale. Crossdykes defend the fort on the east side.

Smacam Down, Cerne Abbas (OS 194; SY 658993).

Rectangular Celtic fields are visible on the slopes to the west of the A352 between Cerne Abbas and Nether Cerne. They are best seen from a distance — the road, or the adjacent hillspur where there is a footpath. On the summit there are traces of a settlement which may have been occupied in Romano-British times. There are similar earthworks on both sides of the Cerne valley, not to be confused with medieval strip lynchets.

Spettisbury Rings or Crawford Castle, Spetisbury (OS 195; ST 915020).

From this small univallate fort, low down and overlooking the Stour valley and Spetisbury village, Badbury Rings is visible. Strengthening of the ramparts was never finished, suggesting a hasty response to the Roman invasion. When a cutting of the Somerset and Dorset Railway (now disused) was excavated in 1857, a cemetery was found containing over a hundred skeletons, probably related to the Roman conquest in AD 43-5.

Swyre Head, Chaldon Herring (OS 194; SY 795805).

Good examples of Celtic fields can be seen on the steep chalk pastures near Swyre Head on the Dorset coast. A visit is best combined with a walk on the coast path from Lulworth Cove.

Valley of Stones, Littlebredy (OS 194; SY 598878).

Celtic and later field systems can be traced on both sides of this dry valley, best seen looking north from the minor road to Abbotsbury from the Hardy Monument. The stones lie among the grass close to the road, and it is likely that this was the source of stones for the nearby megalithic tombs and circles.

ROMAN PERIOD
Ackling Dyke, Oakley Down to Shapwick (OS 184; SU 022178 to OS 195; ST 938017).

This is the Roman road from Old Sarum to Badbury Rings and beyond. From the Dorset border, the modern A354 follows it before deviating and leaving a most spectacular section on Oakley Down. Much of its course can be followed to Badbury Rings, over fine country, crossing the Dorset Cursus and passing barrows and settlement sites. There was a crossroads and small Romano-British settlement outside Badbury Rings, from where a modern lane follows a straight section to Shapwick.

Badbury Rings.

The Cerne Abbas Giant.

Cerne Abbas Giant, Cerne Abbas (OS 194; ST 666016). National Trust.

This famous chalk-cut nude figure is 180 feet (55 m) high and is best viewed from the A352 just north of the village. It is strongly Celtic in style and is believed to be a Romano-British representation of Hercules. He carries a club in his right hand, and a cloak may have hung from his outstretched left arm. Such a large figure must have a ritual significance. On the hill above is the Trendle, which may be related to the Giant. Maypoles were erected in this rectangular earthwork in more recent times.

Dorchester (OS 194; SY 690905).

The *Durnovaria* of Roman Britain, Dorchester was founded in about AD 70. Traces of the Roman town are being discovered continually and the County Museum (chapter 7) contains many finds, including mosaics. One, found at a foundry in 1927, was from a room with an apse and depicts the head of Oceanus, flanked by dolphins and fish. The course of the town walls can be followed by tree-lined walks. A slight bank can be detected, but a small portion of Roman masonry survives at the junction of West Walks and Albert Road. The layout of a fourth-century town house can be seen at Colliton Park, in the north-west corner of the Roman town. This includes two small rooms with hypocausts and a mosaic. Among the excavated finds displayed in the County Museum are a carved shale table leg and a glass bowl engraved with dancing figures.

Dorchester Aqueduct, Dorchester (OS 194; SY 672912).

An aqueduct brought water to Roman Dorchester from the river Frome at Frampton. A well preserved section of the aqueduct can be seen from the Dorchester bypass between the A35 and A37 in Fordington Bottom.

Hod Hill Fort, Stourpaine (OS 194; ST 855107). National Trust.

An 11 acre (4 ha) fort was placed inside the north-west corner of the iron age hillfort. It housed both infantry and cavalry, from soon after the conquest for perhaps twenty years. The defensive earthworks with their two entrances are easily traced.

Jordan Hill Temple, Overcombe (OS 194; SY 700821). English Heritage.

The rectangular foundations of a fourth-century temple are exposed in a field behind a housing development, overlooking Weymouth Bay. When excavated in 1931-2, a shaft was found in the south-east corner, containing ritual deposits of bird bones and bronze coins, placed between flat stones. There were also stone cists with pottery, a sword and a spearhead. Because of its coastal location, the building could have served as a signal station.

Maiden Castle Temple, Dorchester (OS 194; SY 671884). English Heritage.

This temple was built just after AD 367 in the north-east part of the abandoned Maiden

Castle, overlooking Dorchester. Double square foundations represent an inner temple, surrounded by a wall. Downslope are the probable foundations of a two-roomed priest's house.

Maumbury Rings, Dorchester (OS 194; SY 690899).

Close to a crossroads and railway bridge on the road out of Dorchester to Weymouth, and easily missed, are the grassy banks of an amphitheatre. It was built outside the south gate of the Roman town, adapted from an earlier neolithic henge. It saw use in the Civil War and was a place of public executions until 1767.

POST-ROMAN AND SAXON PERIOD

Bokerley Dyke, Cranborne Chase (OS 184; SU 032199 to SU 055181).

The Roman Ackling Dyke and the A354 converge at the Dorset border, where this major earthwork crosses. It is about 4 miles (6 km) long and is mainly a bank and ditch cutting across the natural routeway from the north-east into the rich farmlands of this part of Dorset. At least three stages have been recognised, all related to the troubled fourth century. At times the bank was carried over the Roman road to block it. It is very likely that Bokerley Dyke was used in post-Roman times against Saxon incursion. It is best viewed from the Hampshire side, where there is a nature reserve and car park beside the A354.

Combs Ditch, Winterborne Whitechurch (OS 194; ST 851022 to ST 886001).

This linear earthwork crosses the A354 about 3 miles (5 km) south-west of Blandford Forum. It consists of a low bank and ditch, which can be traced in several places. Not as large or well known as Bokerley Dyke, it served a similar function and may be of a similar date, or much earlier.

Wareham town defences, Wareham (OS 195; 920874).

Wareham became one of King Alfred's burhs towards the end of the ninth century. Although adapted in later times, three sides of the massive Saxon defensive bank and ditch survive today. Wareham was a key site, between the rivers Frome and Piddle at the head of Poole Harbour. The Danes wintered here in AD 877, before being defeated by Alfred in the following year. Wareham is known to have been inhabited in pre-Saxon times, and there is some evidence from excavations that at least the western defences might have existed in some form before the Saxons came.

The Roman wall, Dorchester.

Corfe Castle.

4
Castles and later fortifications

Of all the medieval castles in Dorset, Corfe is the finest and best known. However, there are several smaller but interesting sites where only earthworks remain. These include good early Norman motte and bailey earthworks at **East Chelborough** and **Powerstock,** both in the west of the county. In the north, **Shaftesbury** Castle was probably a temporary work, set up during the twelfth-century civil war between Stephen and Matilda. The site is superb, at the end of its greensand escarpment, but the earthworks fail to impress. In the Blackmoor Vale, some masonry survives at the so-called **Sturminster Newton** 'Castle', although this is part of a fourteenth-century manor house once belonging to Glastonbury Abbey. Facing the medieval bridge over the Stour, it is built on a spur, believed to have once been an iron age defensive work.

Just east of **Gillingham** are the well preserved moat and banks known as King's Court Palace. This was a fortified royal hunting lodge of the early twelfth century and continued in use until 1369, when the buildings were demolished. A bridleway crosses the site from King's Court Road. **Marshwood** Castle was a moated house of the de Mandevilles in the thirteenth century. Only traces survive at Lodge Home Farm, in the Marshwood Vale. In contrast, the rambling **Woodsford** Castle in

the Frome valley east of Dorchester is still inhabited. This fortified house dates from 1337.

Castles are normally associated with the medieval period, but Dorset's two large harbours at Poole and Portland received defensive works during the reign of Henry VIII. Later, in the 1860s, major coastal defences were constructed to protect the naval anchorage in Portland Harbour from a possible French threat. Their scale was unlike anything that had gone before. Dubbed the 'Palmerston follies', they have left substantial remains, particularly on Portland itself. Similar works are found in the areas around the naval bases at Devonport, Portsmouth, Milford Haven, and the Medway and Thames.

CASTLES
Brownsea Castle or Branksea Castle, Brownsea Island. National Trust.

Henry VIII built a blockhouse here in the 1540s, commanding the entrance channel of Poole Harbour. By the early eighteenth century the castle had become a residence. The greatest changes were made after 1765 by Sir Humphrey Sturt of More Crichel, who built a four-storey 'castle', using the earlier one as a base. Two wings were also added. A gatehouse and elaborate pier were added in the

22

nineteenth century. A disastrous fire in 1896 destroyed the interior of the castle, but it was refurbished by 1901. The castle is not open to the public but let to the John Lewis Partnership as a holiday centre.

Christchurch Castle and Constable's House, Christchurch. English Heritage.

All that remains of the castle are two thick stone walls of the Norman keep, on a mound between Castle Street and Church Street. The castle was built by Richard de Redvers in the twelfth century. It was captured by the Parliamentarians in 1645 and dismantled five years later. Nearby is the Constable's House, of which a substantial part remains. It dates from about 1160 and was intended as the residence of the Constable and important guests. Baldwin de Redvers was the builder, and King Edward VI is known to have paid several visits. The main hall was on the first floor. An early fireplace and chimney survive. Note the garderobe projecting over the millstream.

Corfe Castle, Purbeck. Telephone: Corfe Castle (0929) 480921. National Trust.

One of England's great castle ruins, Corfe stands in a classic site on a knoll guarding the routes channelled through a gap in the Purbeck Hills. Here King Edward the Martyr was murdered on the orders of his stepmother in AD 978. A Norman castle was established on the summit by the beginning of the twelfth century, with a square keep surrounded by a bailey. The castle became a gruesome prison during King John's reign. Extension of the castle to its present form was completed by Edward I. The middle and outer baileys were constructed with projecting round towers, and the steep slopes below made the site virtually impregnable. A mansion was built next to the keep, within an enlarged inner bailey, by King John, probably between 1207 and 1214. The castle came into private hands in Elizabethan times. During the Civil War it was held by Lady Bankes against a long siege by the Parliamentary forces, and it was surrendered only by treachery in February 1646. The castle was deliberately blown up. Note the alarming angle at which some of the outer towers lean.

Lulworth Castle, East Lulworth.

This splendid square building with round corner towers was completed in Purbeck stone by about 1608 for Thomas Howard. Hardly a true castle, it was burnt out in 1929. The crumbling and dangerous shell has been closed to the public, but it is visible from a distance. Restoration work has been undertaken to make the castle safe.

Portland Castle, Castletown, Portland. English Heritage.

This well preserved castle is hidden behind present-day military installations on the north shore of Portland. It was built in 1539-40 to protect Portland Roads, and was part of Henry VIII's coastal defence system. Characteristically, its seaward face has low, thick walls, and rounded parapets, with circular walled emplacements for five main guns. Some of the stone is said to have been plundered from Bindon Abbey, near Wool. The castle was taken from the Royalists early in the Civil War but was recaptured after a few months and held until 1646. The final siege lasted eight months, and the castle was the last Royalist stronghold to surrender in Dorset. Afterwards the castle continued in use for coastal defence and was occupied until the nineteenth century.

Rufus Castle, Wakeham, Portland. Also called Bow and Arrow Castle, this was, by local

Christchurch Castle.

tradition, built by William Rufus, although the present ruins probably date from the fifteenth century. It may have been a blockhouse to control Church Ope, a landing place on the east coast of Portland. The castle is private but can be seen from vantage points. Pennsylvania Castle was built nearby in 1800 for John Penn, the Governor of Portland. This large house is now a hotel.

Sandsfoot Castle, Wyke Regis, Weymouth.

This was built in 1541 on the mainland shore to complement Portland Castle, fire from both being able to cover the anchorage in Portland Roads. It is now very ruinous, mainly because of erosion by the sea. The gun emplacements have been lost, but parts of the entrance and living quarters remain.

Sherborne Castle, Castleton, Sherborne. English Heritage.

This is Dorset's second most important castle ruin. It was established in the early twelfth century by Bishop Roger of Old Sarum. The defences have retained much of their earlier appearance, as little was done to take account of improved military ideas. Early in the Civil War the castle was held for the Royalists by Lord Hertford and five hundred men against a force of seven thousand. It was taken by storm. After the war much stone was robbed for buildings in the town, but a surprising amount remains. The outer ward is surrounded by a ditch and the most prominent feature is the partially restored gatehouse. The foundations of the barbican at the north gate show that entry was through a long, stepped passage. Within the castle, some of the keep and living quarters stand to a good height, with finely dressed ashlar as well as decorated Norman arched windows. The new Sherborne Castle lies across the artificial lake to the south (chapter 5).

LATER FORTIFICATIONS: THE PORTLAND HARBOUR DEFENCES

Breakwater Fort, Outer Breakwater.

Part of a complex begun in 1849, the fort (known locally as Chequer Fort) was completed in 1872 at the north end of the Outer Breakwater of Portland Harbour. It is armour-plated, on a Portland stone, granite and concrete base, with a diameter of 116 feet (35 m). It is Ministry of Defence property but can be viewed from the sea. True islands forts of this type were built in the Spithead to protect Portsmouth Dockyard. In 1914 the battleship *Hood* was deliberately sunk in the harbour as an anti-torpedo barrier and is still there.

Nothe Fort, Barrack Road, Weymouth. Telephone: Weymouth (0305) 787243. Weymouth Civic Society.

On the promontory, beyond Nothe Gardens on the south side of Weymouth harbour entrance, Nothe Fort was built in 1860-72, mainly of Portland roach stone, brick and granite. It served a defensive purpose until 1956. Today it is open to the public as a museum of coastal defence. Displays show the three phases of activity here: the Victorian period, First World War and Second World War. There are massive cannons and lighter guns of the twentieth century. Weymouth's close link with the Royal Navy is depicted in models and other items including a torpedo.

Verne Citadel, Portland.

Though it is now a prison, the exterior of the citadel can be viewed on the south side, with its bridge and massive surrounding ditch. The stone quarried here was used for the Portland Breakwater. Before the 1860s, when construction work began, this appears to have been the site of an iron age fort, at the highest point on the island. Nearby is the High Angle Battery, where guns were hidden from the sea and enemy ships. Gun emplacements, underground magazines and tramways have been tidied up for public view.

The gardens at Athelhampton.

5
Historic buildings and gardens

Dorset has a wealth of historic manor houses and other fine buildings. Although not all are open to the public, many can be viewed from nearby and often in a beautiful setting. Others may be opened only occasionally each year, such as **Kingston Maurward,** near Dorchester, which is now the Dorset College of Agriculture, but part of this eighteenth-century house and the formal and teaching gardens are open on four days a year. Some houses are open as part of other attractions, such as **Merley House** and **Compton House** (chapters 7 and 8). Openings are usually confined to the summer, and while some open on only a few days per week they will all reward the effort of visiting.

Abbotsbury Sub-tropical Gardens, Abbotsbury. Telephone: Abbotsbury (030 587) 387.

The gardens are west of the village, beside the road to Chesil Beach. Although so close to the sea, they are protected from the prevailing wind by a hill and a curtain of trees. The gardens were begun in 1760 and extended to 20 acres (8 ha) in the following century. The centre, where peacocks may be seen, is a walled garden, with azaleas, camellias and rhododendrons providing the main colour. Beyond, sub-tropical plants thrive in the shel-

tered environment, and a feature has been made of a small brook. Mature woodlands provide walks around the perimeter.

Athelhampton Hall, near Puddletown. Telephone: Puddletown (030 584) 363.

This is among the great English medieval houses, close to the A35 just east of Puddletown. It is said to be on the site of Athelstan's palace. The main body of this superb stone house was built in the late fifteenth century by Sir William Martyn. He built the Great Hall and a service range with a small corner turret. The hall has the main entrance porch and a notable oriel window at one end. Inside there is original timberwork, including a unique roof. The sturdy, many-windowed west wing was added in the following century and lies at an angle at variance with the rest of the house. Later additions of most periods help lend a rambling air to the rear of the house. Rooms on view include the Great Hall, King's Room and State Bedroom, all with fascinating furnishings. In the grounds is a fine circular dovecote, with mellowed stone and a tiled roof. The formal gardens to the east of the house are broken into distinct walled or hedged areas, with fountains, pools and statuary as common features. There are many world-wide species here, while a group of twelve huge yew pyramids is unforgettable.

Chettle House, Chettle, Blandford Forum. Telephone: Tarrant Hinton (025 889) 209.

Chettle House is the dominant building in the tiny village off the A354 Blandford Forum to Salisbury road. It was designed by Thomas Archer and built in about 1710 for George Chafin, MP and Ranger of Cranborne Chase. It is a tall red-brick building with stone dressings and is a fine example of English baroque. A distinction is achieved by the rounded end bays and west entrance. Alterations were made in the mid nineteenth century, and balustraded parapets were added to the wings in 1912. Some ground-floor rooms are open to the public. A wooden staircase in two flights makes an interesting feature in the East Hall. Works by contemporary painters are displayed in a fine art gallery. Outside, the semi-formal gardens and a small nursery garden are also open.

Clouds Hill, Bovington. National Trust.

Surrounded by woodland and heathland to the north of Bovington Camp, this tiny cottage was owned for ten years by T. E. Lawrence (Lawrence of Arabia), until his fatal motorcycle accident near Wool in 1935. There are few windows and its dark interior contains sparse furnishings, giving the feel of a retreat. There are some interesting photographs on display. Lawrence is buried at Moreton, across the river Frome. At Wareham, his effigy is in St Martin's church and items of interest are in the museum.

T. E. Lawrence's grave at Moreton.

Compton Acres Gardens, Canford Cliffs, Poole. Telephone: Canford Cliffs (0202) 700778.

This is said to be one of the finest gardens in Europe, created since 1919 as the brainchild of Thomas W. Simpson. Nine individual gardens are included in the 15 acres (6 ha) of this sheltered site overlooking Poole Harbour. The Japanese Garden, created by Japanese workers, may be the only genuine garden of its type in Europe. The other gardens include the Italian, Rock and Water, Heather, Palm Court, Roman and Herbaceous gardens. Bronze and marble statues feature prominently in the gardens.

Cranborne Manor Gardens, Cranborne. Telephone: Cranborne (07254) 248.

These historic gardens were laid out in the seventeenth century by John Tradescant and enlarged in the twentieth century. Walls and yew hedges surround the White, Herb, Mount and Knot gardens, and there are also water and wild gardens. The gardens open on Wednesdays in spring and summer but the garden centre is open at most times.

Deans Court Garden, Wimborne Minster.

There are 13 acres (5 ha) of partly wild garden beside the river Allen, tucked away and easily missed just south of the Minster and town centre. There is a fishpond, a kitchen garden with a serpentine wall, and the Henry Doubleday Research Association sanctuary for threatened vegetables.

Edmondsham House and Gardens, near Cranborne. Telephone: Cranborne (07254) 207.

Descendants of Lewis Tregonwell, the founder of Bournemouth, live in the house, which is a mixture of Tudor and Georgian styles with a Victorian stable block and dairy. This family home is open occasionally but the surrounding gardens are open during the summer months. There are lawns, shrubs and a walled garden, which is managed organically.

Fiddleford Mill House, Sturminster Newton. English Heritage.

Here are a hall and solar dating from a rebuilding of the mid fourteenth century, located at the south end of a stone-built range now occupied as a farmhouse. The building has been restored in modern times. The decorated roof timbers are a major feature. Fiddleford is in an idyllic setting, beside the Stour and the weir for the disused Fiddleford Mill (where an inscription is dated 1556). A good approach is on foot, across the fields from Sturminster Newton. Fiddleford was a staging point on the eighteenth-century smugglers' route from the coast.

The Japanese Garden, Compton Acres.

Forde Abbey, Thorncombe, near Chard. Telephone: South Chard (0460) 20231.

This house of Ham stone is on the site of a Cistercian abbey, beside the river Axe and close to the Somerset border. The front lawn has replaced the church, but other parts of the abbey are incorporated in the house. The twelfth-century chapter house is now a chapel, and the thirteenth-century dorter range also survives. The great attraction is the early sixteenth-century Abbot's Hall with its high porch, ornately carved and with tall windows. The north side of the cloister is of similar date and now forms a conservatory. In 1649 Sir Edmond Prideaux created a home by making alterations to the hall and building a large saloon. Much of the house remains little altered since that time. The whole is crenellated and the plaster ceilings within are very fine. There are also tapestries of note. There are about 30 acres (12 ha) of garden, with mature shrubs and trees, rock and water gardens, and a kitchen garden. An arboretum dates from the post-war years.

Kingston Lacy House, near Wimborne Minster. Telephone: Wimborne (0202) 883402. National Trust.

When Henry Ralph Bankes died in 1981, he bequeathed 16,000 acres (6400 ha) to the National Trust, which included this house, Badbury Rings, Corfe Castle and the coast and heaths at Studland. After extensive restoration work, Kingston Lacy was opened to the public in 1986. The house was built in 1663-5 for Sir Ralph Bankes and was designed by Sir Roger Pratt (the first architect to be knighted). In the 1830s Sir Charles Barry altered the appearance by facing the brick walls with Chilmark stone. He added a robust chimney to each corner and lowered the entrance to basement level. Within, the library has an important collection of books as well as the old keys to Corfe Castle. There are statues by Baron Marochetti, and the paintings include the works of several great masters. In the park is an Egyptian obelisk from Philae, erected here in 1827. To the north-west, a 2 mile (3 km) avenue of beeches lines the B3082 as it passes Badbury Rings (chapter 3).

Knoll Gardens, Stapehill Road, Wimborne. Telephone: Wimborne (0202) 873931.

Worldwide exotic shrubs and plants, rockeries, water gardens, waterfalls and ponds, including a large Australian plant collection, make these gardens delightful to visit.

Mapperton Gardens, Mapperton, Beaminster. Telephone: Beaminster (0308) 862645.

Set at the head of a secluded valley, these are the grounds of Mapperton Manor (open to organised parties), which has Tudor origins, with additions in the seventeenth and eighteenth centuries. There are terraced and hillside gardens with daffodils, formal borders, specimen shrubs and trees. Other features include fishponds, a summerhouse and an orangery.

Forde Abbey.

Milton Abbey House, Milton Abbas.

Next to Milton Abbey (chapter 6), this eighteenth-century mansion was designed by Sir William Chambers for Joseph Damer, Earl of Dorchester. It is rather formal in style and makes use of coursed pale limestone and flints. Now a public school, the King's Room, Library and Ball Room are open during summer holidays. There are Adam fireplaces and ceilings by James Wyatt. The Abbot's Hall of 1498, with an original ceiling and screen, is also incorporated in the complex of buildings. The grounds were laid out by Capability Brown.

Minterne Gardens, Minterne House, Minterne Magna. Telephone: Cerne Abbas (030 03) 370.

This is a sheltered site at the upper end of the Cerne valley, with mature trees and shrubs. The gardens include lakes with streams and cascades, and there are long walks amongst rhododendrons, azaleas, magnolias and hydrangeas.

Parnham, Beaminster. Telephone: Beaminster (0308) 862204.

This embattled and pinnacled stone house lies off the A3066 Bridport road, just south of Beaminster. It is now the home of the John Makepeace Furniture Workshops and School for Craftsmen. The original fifteenth-century house of the Strode family was rebuilt by them in the following century. The Great Hall survives, despite alterations in the mid eighteenth century and the finishing touches added by John Nash in 1810. Great care has been taken to restore the interior of this grand house. In the grounds there are 14 acres (6 ha) of varied gardens from the formal to the informal. Use is made of water, with cascades next to the steps to the Great Lawn, while there are quieter walks beside the river Brit. The Yew Terrace includes topiary. The Working Woodland is 3 miles (4.8 km) away at Hooke Park, where the School for Woodland Industry teaches the efficient use of timber resources. Displays, an unusual building and woodland walks are open to the public.

Purse Caundle Manor, near Sherborne. Telephone: Milborne Port (0963) 250400.

This attractive manor house dates from the fifteenth and sixteenth centuries. Rooms open to the public include the Great Hall, with a minstrel gallery, the winter parlour, solar and bedchambers.

Sandford Orcas Manor, Sandford Orcas, Sherborne. Telephone: Corton Denham (096 322) 206.

The village is lost among lanes below an escarpment, just north of Sherborne and almost in Somerset. The manor presents a fine example of Tudor architecture behind a gatehouse, all in golden Ham stone. Within, the house contains Queen Anne furniture, stained glass and paintings of interest. Outside, there are terraced and walled gardens. The church (St Nicholas) is part of the same group of buildings and contains monuments to the Knoyle family of the manor.

Sherborne Castle, Castleton, Sherborne. Telephone: Sherborne (0935) 813182.

This is sometimes known as New Sherborne Castle, to avoid confusion with the earlier one. It was built by Sir Walter Raleigh in 1594, with four corner turrets. It has been owned by the Digbys ever since 1617, when Sir John Digby added four wings and towers, with balustrades and many chimneys. The bizarre appearance is reinforced by plain rendering of the walls, although dressings of Ham stone remain uncovered. The interior was redecorated in the mid nineteenth century, although the Red Drawing Room retains a period plaster ceiling. To the south, the house looks out over fields and woodland, with no other house in sight. Capability Brown landscaped the park, which features a large lake between the new and old castles. At its far end is Pinford Bridge. Curiosities in the grounds include Sir Walter Raleigh's Seat, said to be where his servant drenched his master to put out the pipe he was smoking. Behind the house is a neo-classical orangery of 1779; the Gothick dairy (now a tea room) contains a Roman mosaic. Beside the entrance drive, the stable block with two wings is notable for its huge proportions.

Smedmore House, Kimmeridge. Telephone: Corfe Castle (0929) 480717.

This is a manor house, begun by Sir William Clavell in the early seventeenth century. Later alterations in the 1760s added twin bows to the front. The house contains Dutch paintings and furniture and a collection of antique dolls. There are also photographs and documents concerning the house. The grounds include walled flower and vegetable gardens and a herb court. The house is secluded with trees, just to the east of the attractive village of Kimmeridge.

Tudor House, 3 Trinity Street, Weymouth. Telephone: Weymouth (0305) 789742. Weymouth Civic Society.

This is the only early seventeenth-century merchant's town house in Weymouth open to the public. It is faced in Portland stone and the interior has furnishings of the period.

Upton Park, Upton, near Poole. Telephone: Poole (0202) 672628. Poole Borough Council.

Upton Country Park surrounds a wealthy Poole merchant's house of about 1818. The hall, chapel and other ground floor rooms of this attractive house are open on most Sunday afternoons. There are landscaped formal gardens and woodland, parkland and shoreline

Parnham.

The new Sherborne Castle was begun in 1594 by Sir Walter Raleigh.

trails. The park looks over Hole's Bay and Pergins Island. The Countryside Heritage Centre in the old stable block contains an historic wildfowling punt and exhibitions on the natural history of heathland and shore.

Wolfeton House, Charminster. Telephone: Dorchester (0305) 63500.

Isolated to the south of Charminster village, where the Cerne meets the Frome, this is a romantic house of mellowed Purbeck stone. It dates mainly from the sixteenth century, and its builders were the Trenchards, who are commemorated in Charminster's church. The earliest features are the gatehouse and two towers. The latter, one round and the other octagonal, give an almost French appearance to the house. Inside, the Great Hall, ceilings, stairs and fireplaces are all of note. Visitors are given a taste of home-produced cider, made in the cider house, where traditional equipment can be seen and cider purchased. Close by, but not open to the public, is a large barn which is the earliest surviving riding school in England, dating from about 1610.

Norman carving on the north turret at Christchurch Priory.

6
Churches

THE GREAT CHURCHES

Christchurch Priory: Holy Trinity.

This is the longest parish church in England, at 311 feet (95 m). Even the north porch may be the longest. The first known church dates from the mid seventh century, but the Priory church was begun in 1094 by Ranulf Flambard, later Bishop of Durham.

Externally, the Priory is of great interest, showing several phases of development. Of special note is the decorated north turret, with Romanesque blind arches. Above the early fifteenth-century Lady Chapel is St Michael's Loft, once a school and now a museum. The west tower is late fifteenth century. Note the Christchurch salmon weathervane, erected in 1969. There was once a central tower with a spire but they collapsed in a storm in about 1420. A small carving depicting the spire can be seen above the door of the Draper Chantry (John Draper was the last prior, in 1520-39).

The nave, completed by 1150, is one of the finest in England. It has massive pillars, with geometric carvings above the arches. Upper double arches form the triforium. At the crossing, the nave screen dates from about 1320 and includes tiny carvings of animals. The Great Quire is raised. The Jesse reredos or altar screen is of mid fourteenth-century date.

It shows Christ's family tree and is a fine piece of workmanship. There are old misericords in the choir stalls, including one of 1210, the earliest known in England. There is a tomb chest with much defaced alabaster effigies of Sir John and Lady Katherine Chidiock (1461). The ornate Salisbury Chantry, probably by an Italian sculptor, was erected as a tomb for Margaret, Countess of Salisbury. However, she was beheaded and buried at the Tower of London in 1541. In the Montacute Chapel (north transept) is the obscure Apostles Pillar, showing a two-faced Judas. Beneath the west tower is the fine white marble memorial to Percy Bysshe Shelley, who drowned in the Gulf of Spezia in 1822 and whose ashes are buried at Rome.

High up in the south choir aisle, the Miraculous Beam protrudes through an arch. Legend has it that this roof timber was cut a foot too short, but overnight it was lengthened and put in place with plenty to spare. The unseen workman could only have been Christ, and this is how the church and town gained their name.

Milton Abbey: St Mary, St Michael, St Sampson and St Branwalader.

Of the four great churches, this alone is in a rural setting. A college of secular priests was founded here in AD 934 by King Athelstan. It became a Benedictine monastery, which grew until the Dissolution in 1539. Ham and Chilmark stone was brought in, with local flint used for lesser walls. The Dissolution prevented the nave from being built, making the church appear unusually tall.

The abbey was bought by Sir John Tregonwell, and the church was used by the village of Milton Abbas until the late eighteenth century. Then Joseph Damer (later Earl of Dorchester) created the new model village with its own church, in order to erase the old village to landscape his property. The abbey church is now used by the public school which occupies Damer's Milton Abbey House. The cruciform church seen today dates from the fourteenth and fifteenth centuries, when it was rebuilt after a destructive fire in 1309. Within, the architecture is especially fine. The reredos of 1492 is of note, and there is a rare wooden pyx, with four storeys and a spire. Monuments include a Purbeck marble altar tomb to Sir John Tregonwell (1565). His descendants were to found Bournemouth. The most eyecatching monument is in the north transept. This is a white marble work, depicting the reclining Countess of Dorchester with her husband beside, gazing into her face. This unusual effigy is by A. Carlini, and the tomb by Robert Adam (1775). At the top of a long flight of grass steps to the east of the church is St Catherine's Chapel, which has Norman origins.

Sherborne Abbey: St Mary.

Considered by some to be Dorset's finest church, Sherborne Abbey is resplendent in golden Ham stone with the feel of a cathedral. A cathedral church was founded here in about AD 705, when St Aldhelm became the first bishop. The diocese was transferred to Old Sarum in 1075. Small traces of the Saxon church can be seen, but much was rebuilt in the twelfth century, by which time a Benedictine monastery had been established. There was friction between the monastery and the town, which grew until the abbey church was seriously damaged by a fire in the fifteenth century. The legacy of the rebuilding work is the graceful and intricate fan vaulting of the tall nave and choir, for which the church is best known. Norman work survives in the tower and transepts, while the south door has a fine Norman archway. After the Dissolution in 1539, the town acquired the church from Sir John Horsey. There are good fifteenth-century misericords, which repay a close inspection, and there is painted glass of similar date in the Leweston Chapel. Two Purbeck marble effigies of twelfth and thirteenth-century abbots are reminders of the abbey. The sixteenth-century canopied tombs of the Horseys and Lewestons are very fine. The effigies of Sir John Horsey and his son (1546 and 1564, both armoured) are especially well preserved. Much of one wall of the south transept is taken up by the baroque monument to John Digby, Earl of Bristol, with two wives (1698). This

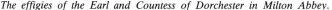

The effigies of the Earl and Countess of Dorchester in Milton Abbey.

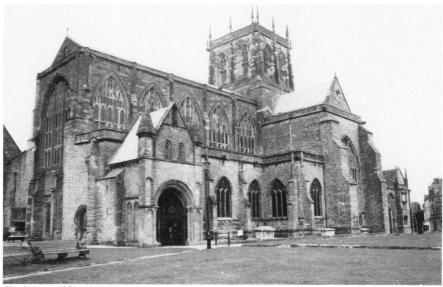

Sherborne Abbey.

was designed by John Nost, whose fine monument to Sir Hugh Wyndham is in Silton church.

Wimborne Minster: St Cuthberga.
There has been a church at Wimborne since AD 713, when a nunnery was founded by Cuthberga, sister of King Ine. King Aethelred of the West Saxons was killed in battle with the Danes near Bokerley Dyke in AD 871 and is thought to be buried here. The present minster, with its two towers, contains much of interest. Outside, the use of red heathstone and pale limestone is striking. There is also greensand in the west tower. The central tower and nave are mainly Norman, while the church was later extended and widened in the thirteenth and fifteenth centuries. A spire on the central tower fell in 1600. Beneath the west tower is an octagonal font of Purbeck marble, but here is also the early fourteenth-century astronomical clock, which shows the sun and moon orbiting the earth. Outside on the north side is the quarter-jack, a colourful figure which strikes a bell at each quarter hour. The alabaster Beaufort tomb is of note. Look for the tomb of Anthony Ettricke, who had his coffin placed under an arch in the wall. He lived beyond the expected date of his death, so the date on the tomb had to be altered to 1703. It was Ettricke who committed the Duke of Monmouth for trial when he was captured near Horton in 1685. The crypt is very fine, and there is also a chained library, where rare

books can be consulted but not removed. A large sundial of 1676, formerly on the gable of the south transept, was re-erected below the west tower in 1894.

COUNTRY CHURCHES
One of the great joys of the Dorset countryside is the wealth of delightful churches. They may be remote, or in villages and small hamlets which are worthy of a visit in themselves. The Dorset Historic Churches Trust is active in preservation, while the Redundant Churches Fund administers some churches no longer required for worship, but of great architectural interest. The following is a selection but nearly every church has something of interest and few will disappoint. Some other churches in towns and villages are described in chapter 10.

Batcombe: St Mary. A humble fifteenth-century church nestles below the steep escarpment of the north Dorset downs, best seen from the road along the crest above.

Bere Regis: St John the Baptist. This important Dorset church is of Norman origin, but much reconstructed. Outside, the robust tower is of flint and ashlar chequer work. Inside, Norman pillars have carved capitals with grotesques; one depicts a bearded man with a headache. The most striking feature is the late fifteenth-century timber roof spanning the nave. It has large carved figures of the twelve

Apostles. The Turberville crypt is below the chapel in the south aisle. This is significant in Thomas Hardy's *Tess of the d'Urbervilles* (chapter 9).

Buckland Newton: Holy Rood. The church stands apart from a scattered village, with an unusual exterior of pale rendering. The interior is plain, with some interesting details. Stone corbel heads in the thirteenth-century chancel may represent Henry III, his queen, the bishop, the lord and lady of the manor, and the church mason. There is an Elizabethan baptismal robe on the north wall. Over the south door is a sculptured fragment of unusual style, found in the vicarage garden in 1926. Certainly as old as the early ninth century, it is a puzzle and may represent a warrior, St Thomas or Christ.

Canford Magna: unknown dedication. This is important for surviving parts of the Saxon church, but the whole was much altered over subsequent centuries. The village is overpowered by the public school.

Chalbury: unknown dedication. This tiny chapel with a white exterior stands on a hilltop which is a surprisingly good viewpoint, looking down on the eighteenth-century Horton Tower and all round. It is probably thirteenth-century, but there is an interesting Georgian interior with box pews and a timbered entry to the chancel. There are two fonts.

Charminster: St Mary. This lovely church has an exterior of limestone and Ham stone. Inside, pale stone was used for the Norman chancel arch and round pillars with transitional arches in the nave. Note the damaged table tombs of the Trenchards in the south chapel. Here is also Grace Pole's monument (1678), colourful with a kneeling figure at prayer and pink cherubs in the clouds above. There are fifteenth-century stone corbels with heads for the nave roof. Sir Thomas Trenchard of Wolfeton is believed to have built the sixteenth-century tower, where his monogram of interwined Ts is carved.

Cranborne: St Mary and St Bartholemew. There was a small abbey here from about AD 980 until 1102, when the monks moved to Tewkesbury. Cranborne remained a dependent priory until 1540. The present church was rebuilt in the thirteenth century, and the large, robust tower was added two hundred years later. The chancel was rebuilt in 1875, but the nave survives in the Early English style. There are contemporary wall paintings above the south arcade, dated to about 1240. Bare legs, feet, fish and a staff are all that remains of St Christopher. Another painting depicts The Doom, with a tree growing from a woman's head, showing the seven deadly sins. The octagonal font of Purbeck marble is of the same date. Wall monuments include one with the figure of a seated boy. This was John Elliot of Cornwall, considered a genius when he died suddenly at school in Cranborne in 1641. Two-seater pews on the south side are unusual.

Gussage St Andrew: Originally the chapel of a nunnery, now behind a large farmhouse, the church is a simple building, mainly twelfth- and thirteenth-century, of flint with greensand dressings. It is remarkable for thirteenth-

The tiny church at Chalbury has a Georgian interior.

Maiden Newton church contains an original Norman door.

century wall paintings, and there is a twelfth-century font. Lighting is by candles.

Hilton: All Saints. This village church is outstanding for the windows of the north aisle and the fan vault in the porch, both having come from the cloister of nearby Milton Abbey. Other salvaged features include wooden panels with paintings of the Apostles, dated to the twelfth century.

Kingston: St James. The church was built in 1880 to the design of G. E. Street. The tower is a major landmark, high on the escarpment which looks north towards Corfe Castle and Poole Harbour. Local Purbeck stone and marble have been used throughout, to a high standard of workmanship. The dark interior is unlike anything else in the area.

Maiden Newton: St Mary. This is a noteworthy church in a large village in the Frome valley. There is Norman work in the nave and central tower. The south aisle and chancel were added in the fifteenth century. Here is what is believed to be an original Norman door, still hanging on its hinges. Outside, there is interesting stonework, and small heads can be seen on the side of the squat crenellated tower. In the churchyard is the tomb of Hugh Croft, who died in 1725, aged 107 years.

Marnhull: St Gregory the Great. A noble fifteenth-century tower of pale local stone stands out in the Blackmoor Vale. The interior

is large and airy. Sole survivor of the Norman church is a carved capital with three faces in the north arcade. The south arcade is tall and grand, also with carved capitals. Early wall paintings include part of a skeleton with a spade. The Carent tomb (1470) has an alabaster knight lying with a lady on each side, There are traces of paintwork. Note also the rude rectangular font of limestone on a Purbeck marble plinth.

Melbury Bubb: St Mary. Peacefully situated in a tiny hamlet below the wooded Bubb Down Hill, the church's treasure is the carved Saxon font. It is intricately carved, with four large animals, two dragons and a serpent. As they are upside down, it may be a crossbase, reused and hollowed out by the Normans. Much of the church was rebuilt by the Victorians, but the fifteenth-century tower and some late medieval painted glass survive.

Melcombe Horsey: St Andrew. Approached by the drive of Bingham's Melcombe, a beautiful country house, the church is small, mainly fourteenth- and fifteenth-century, and appealing in its situation in this quiet valley. Inside, note the unusually descriptive wall monuments. Grassed-over earthworks on either side of the drive mark the site of the medieval village.

Portland, Reforne: St George. This remarkable Georgian church was designed and built in 1754-66 by Thomas Gilbert, a local man. It stands apart, in a quarry-scarred landscape, with a churchyard of fine tombstones of Portland stone. There is a low central dome and a west tower with a cupola. Inside are period box pews and galleries. This largely unaltered church is in the care of the Redundant Churches Fund.

Powerstock: St Mary. The church suffered Victorian restoration, but the Norman chancel arch is richly carved and very impressive. The fifteenth-century south doorway is also of note. The attractive village is lost among the hills of west Dorset.

Puddletown: St Mary. There is much of interest in this mainly fifteenth-century church. Note the panelled nave roof and the seventeenth-century box pews, gallery and stairs. Bath Sun Fire Office buckets hang beneath the gallery. The beaker-shaped font is richly carved and may be Saxon. The south chapel is a gem. It contains splendid medieval tombs, notably alabaster effigies of a thirteenth-century knight and his lady, and of Sir William Martyn (died 1503) beneath a Purbeck marble canopy.

St Aldhelm's Head Chapel. Boldly placed on St Aldhelm's or St Alban's Head, high above the sea near Worth Matravers, this tiny chapel was built some time in the second half of the twelfth century. There is a Norman arched door, and a central pillar supports the vaulted roof of the dark interior.

Silton: St Nicholas. The mostly fifteenth-century church has a charming exterior of mellowed stone. This contrasts with the interior, where only the tiny north chapel is of architectural note. A monument to Sir Hugh Wyndham dominates the north wall of the nave and is complete with two weeping women. It was erected in 1692 and is a fine example of its kind, but seemingly out of place in this rural church.

Studland: St Nicholas. Here, within sight and sound of the sea, is a religious haven surprisingly little affected by more recent developments around Studland village. The church, with its low, axial tower, is almost pure Norman. Within the dark interior, the chancel arch is very fine. Carvings and grotesques abound, both inside and out. There is a strong period atmosphere, more so than at Worth Matravers.

Sydling St Nicholas. Set apart from the village, on higher ground between a manor house and a farm with an iron-roofed tithe barn, the church was rebuilt in the fifteenth and eighteenth centuries. Outside, there are some fine gargoyles. Plain glass windows give light to the interior, where eighteenth- and nineteenth-century wall monuments are numerous.

Tarrant Crawford: St Mary. This small church of flint and sandstone is delightfully set at the end of a lane, past two large barns. It lies near the site of a former Cistercian nunnery. The

The church at Bingham's Melcombe is typical of many of the smaller Dorset churches.

The Norman church at Studland.

fourteenth-century wall paintings in the nave are the main feature. They include the story of St Margaret of Antioch and the allegory of the Three Living and Three Dead.

Toller Fratrum: St Basil. The Knights Hospitallers of St John of Jerusalem had a priory here. Today there is a farming community, with a small rectangular Victorian church. Within are two unexpected gems. The font is one of the best in Dorset, with powerful carvings of figures, very Celtic in style but possibly of twelfth-century date. Set in the wall behind the altar is a carved fragment of St Mary Magdalene washing Christ's feet, dated to about 1050.

Trent: St Andrew. Trent is almost over the border, with a feel of Somerset, to which the village looks and once belonged. Handsome stone buildings surround the church and its large churchyard. There is a tall tower, with a rebuilt spire of the fourteenth century. Note the carved heads at the top of the tower. Among the wooden fittings are a fine rood screen, a richly carved pulpit and figured bench ends. There are two fourteenth-century effigies. Later memorials include one to Sir Francis Wyndham of Trent House, who hid the future Charles II while he was escaping

from his defeat at the battle of Worcester in 1651. Lord Fisher of Lambeth, the ninety-ninth Archbishop of Canterbury, is buried here.

Whitchurch Canonicorum: St Candida and Holy Cross. This is a large church in the Marshwood Vale. The fine early thirteenth-century carved capitals are of special note. Here is the shrine of St Candida or St Wite, a Saxon holy woman whose bones were found in a lead casket and lie in a stone coffin in the north transept. There are three holes through which pilgrims may pass diseased limbs in the hope of a cure. Among the later monuments is a fine one to Sir John Jeffery (1611).

Whitcombe: unknown dedication. This small church stands alone in a field near a walled farm and cottages, all neatly thatched. The tower is of the sixteenth century, but the nave is mainly twelfth-century. Two richly carved Saxon cross fragments are evidence for its pre-conquest origin. Wall paintings include St Christopher carrying the Christ child on his shoulder. Other details include a mermaid with a mirror. They date from about 1400. The disused church is in the care of the Redundant Churches Fund. It was here that the poet William Barnes began and ended his ministry.

37

He was rector of nearby Winterborne Came, where his grave is marked by a Celtic cross beside the tiny church, lost behind a high wall and overlooking meadows.

Wimborne St Giles. The church was rebuilt in 1732, with exterior walls of flint and greensand chequer work. After a disastrous fire in 1908, it was restored by Sir Ninian Comper, whose most impressive fitting is the long rood screen which crosses the unusually wide interior. There are several memorials to the Ashley Coopers and Earls of Shaftesbury. The largest is to Sir Anthony Ashley (1627). He is said to have first introduced cabbages into England, and a carving at his feet may be a symbolic cabbage! He also built the brick almshouses of 1624, which are attached to the church.

Winterborne Clenston: St Nicholas. This small steepled church of coursed flint and ashlar was designed by Lewis Vulliamy in 1840. It sits neatly on the east side of the lovely Winterborne valley but is more interesting without than within.

Winterborne Tomson: unknown dedication. The single-cell twelfth-century chancel with an apse is unique in the county. After falling into disuse, it was restored in 1936 by A. R. Powys as a memorial to Thomas Hardy. There are eighteenth-century box pews, a gallery and a wagon roof. It is in the care of the Redundant Churches Fund.

Winterborne Whitechurch: St Mary. This lovely church of thirteenth-century origin has a sturdy axial tower and an unusual plan. Inside, carvings on broad capitals have stern faces and are possibly angels. The carved font dates from 1450. John Wesley's grandfather was rector here.

Worth Matravers: St Nicholas of Myra. Although lacking the full Norman feel of Studland, this other Purbeck church has an extremely fine chancel arch, carved with chevrons. This and the nave date from the mid twelfth century. The west tower is slightly later and is capped with a pyramidal roof of 1869. Unlike Studland, the church fits into an attractive stone-built village.

Winterborne Clenston church dates from 1840.

The font at Toller Fratrum is a powerful piece of carving.

7
Museums and galleries

Dorset has a great number of museums of all sizes. They range from Bournemouth's Russell-Cotes Art Gallery and Museum, packed with many exotic exhibits, down to a single eighteenth-century fire engine housed in the village centre at Okeford Fitzpaine, and easily missed. No visit to Dorset is complete without visiting the County Museum in Dorchester, while most of the smaller local museums have their own special treasures. These latter are often manned by enthusiastic volunteers, but opening times may be restricted to the summer months. Intending visitors should find out the opening times before making a special journey.

ARNE
Purbeck Toy and Musical Box Museum, Arne, near Wareham. Telephone: Wareham (0929) 552018.

The World of Toys is in the tiny village of Arne and contains a large selection of Victorian and Edwardian dolls, teddy bears, prams, trains, cars, boats, automated toys and musical boxes.

BLANDFORD FORUM
Blandford Forum Museum, Old Coach House, Bere's Yard, Market Place, Blandford Forum DT11 7HU. Telephone: Blandford (0258) 451115.

This developing museum was officially opened in 1985 and contains much of local interest. There are displays on archaeology, Dorset buttons, militaria, Victoriana and a collection of chimney pots, and the Blandford fire of 1731. A small room is devoted to agricultural bygones. An unusual exhibit is a dynamo which supplied the first domestic electricity in the town.

Royal Signals Museum, School of Signals, Blandford Camp, Blandford Forum DT11 8RH. Telephone: Blandford (0258) 452581, extension 2248.

Comprehensive and well displayed, this is a museum to the history of a vital but little considered aspect of army life. All types of communication equipment are on show. Of particular interest are heliographs as used on the North-west Frontier in the nineteenth century, and a cable wagon drawn by six horses, used from 1905 until the 1930s. Other displays include uniforms, medals and other equipment. There is a reference library with archives. Blandford Camp is suitably placed

on a hill which was a naval telegraph station in 1806-15.

BOURNEMOUTH
Russell-Cotes Art Gallery and Museum, East Cliff, Bournemouth BH1 3AA. Telephone: Bournemouth (0202) 551009.

Housed in a late Victorian mansion of architectural interest on the cliff top, not far from Bournemouth Pier, this was the home of Sir Merton Russell-Cotes, East Cliff Hall. The rooms are sumptuous, with painted ceilings, and the house was presented to the town together with a large collection of art objects. The Japanese collection includes a Buddhist shrine and a suit of armour of very fine work. The museum is packed with items such as paintings, ceramics, sculptures and furniture. Collections of weapons, ship models and shells and the Lucas Collection of paintings have been brought here from the now closed Rothesay Museum. Outside is the Geological Terrace, where blocks of 202 different rocks are displayed next to the public footpath. The new Display Space wing has changing exhibits from the museum's permanent collection.

Shelley Rooms Museum, Boscombe Manor, Shelley Park, Beechwood Avenue, Boscombe, Bournemouth. Telephone: Bournemouth (0202) 303571.

This is the only museum devoted to the poet Percy Bysshe Shelley and includes a small reference library on the romantic period. It is housed in two rooms in the former home of Shelley's son, Sir Percy Florence Shelley, who lived here from 1849 to 1884. The poet's widow, Mary, members of her family and the son are buried in St Peter's churchyard, Bournemouth. The rooms contain a resource centre for local history and literature.

BOVINGTON CAMP
The Tank Museum, Bovington Camp, Wareham BH20 6JG. Telephone: Bindon Abbey (0929) 462721, extensions 329 and 463 or (0929) 463953.

This is the Corps museum of the Royal Armoured Corps and the Regimental museum of the Royal Tank Regiment. It is the largest collection of its type in the world, with over 160 tracked and wheeled armoured fighting vehicles, representative of all periods of development from 1915 to the present. Many

Red House Museum, Christchurch.

nations are represented, including an Argentinian armoured car from the Falklands conflict of 1982. A popular feature is a Centurion tank cut in half to reveal the interior. Displays include uniforms and armaments. The reference library and photographic collection can be visited by appointment. There is a self service restaurant and a bookshop and there are pleasant picnic areas next to the museum. Bovington Camp is the headquarters of the Royal Armoured Corps and the adjacent Wool Heath is a training area for driving tanks and armoured cars. A spectacular open day is held at Gallows Hill every July.

BRIDPORT
Bridport Museum and Art Gallery, South Street, Bridport DT6 3NR. Telephone: Bridport (0308) 22116.

This small museum is housed in an interesting old stone building. There is an important display on ropemaking and netmaking, industries for which the town has long been famous. One 'jumper' netmaking loom was made in Bridport in 1840 and worked until 1968. Upstairs, in the art gallery, is Dr Donald Omand's collection of dolls in international dress. He was a local man who travelled widely and befriended circus folk, who gave him many of the dolls. Other exhibits relate to the history of Bridport and its surroundings.

BURTON BRADSTOCK
Bredy Farm Collection, Bredy Farm, between Litton Cheney and Burton Bradstock.

There is an old farming collection at this working farm in the Bride valley to the east of Burton Bradstock. There are traditional Dorset wagons, cidermaking equipment and a sawmill. Dairying and arable farming are undertaken here, and visitors may watch the milking in the afternoon.

CHRISTCHURCH
Christchurch Tricycle Museum, Priory Car Park, The Quay, Christchurch. Telephone: Highcliffe (042 52) 3240.

This small but interesting museum is devoted to tricycles, with exhibits ranging from a boneshaker tricycle of 1869 to a Pashley 'Panther' of the 1980s. Children's tricycles and a Bath chair are exhibited, while multi-wheeled cycles are represented by a 1935 replica of a five-wheeled Pentacycle, originally invented by Edward Burstow in 1882.

Red House Museum and Art Gallery, Quay Road, Christchurch BH23 1BU. Telephone: Christchurch (0202) 482860.

This attractive red-bricked building is the former eighteenth-century workhouse. Displays tell the story of Christchurch through archaeology and social history, including domestic items. There are new natural history and geology galleries. The costume gallery follows the development of fashionable dress in the period 1865-1915. Temporary exhibitions are also held. Outside, the gardens are peaceful and include a walled herb garden.

Wedgwood Electrical Collection, Bargates, Christchurch. Telephone: Christchurch (0202) 784047.

The collection is in the engine and battery rooms of Southern Electric's former power station. Over five hundred exhibits explain over a century of development of the electricity supply industry. There are generators, switchgear, transformers, domestic appliances, lighting and wiring systems, and replicas of early laboratory equipment. Although only open on Wednesday afternoons in the summer, visitors may telephone for access at other times.

CORFE CASTLE
Corfe Castle Town Trust Museum, West Street, Corfe Castle.

A small museum beneath the old town hall contains items of local interest.

DORCHESTER

Dinosaur Museum, Icen Way, Dorchester DT1 1EW. Telephone: Dorchester (0305) 269880.

This imaginative museum is the only one in Britain devoted to dinosaurs and other archosaurs. There are fossils, footprints and models from the Dorset area and throughout the world. There are novel ways in which visitors can investigate aspects of dinosaurs, including feeling the texture of their skins.

Dorset County Museum, High West Street, Dorchester DT1 1XA. Telephone: Dorchester (0305) 62735.

This is the museum of the Dorset Natural History and Archaeological Society. The centrepiece is a Victorian iron pillared and arched hall. There are various items relating to Thomas Hardy, including a reconstruction of his study. The rural craft collection contains farming and smithy exhibits as well as items used for making Dorset Blue Vinney cheese. The museum's important archaeological collection includes Roman mosaic pavements of the fourth century and a modern prize-winning gallery traces the history of Dorset from the palaeolithic period through to the Romans and beyond, with a theme of the danger to sites from modern land use. Artefacts on display include finds from Maiden Castle and Roman Dorchester. Another gallery is devoted to the natural history of Dorset. There is a good geological collection, with dinosaur footprints, fossilised trees and other fossils, and a small exhibit about the Dorset oil industry. Temporary exhibitions are organised.

Dorset Military Museum, The Keep, Bridport Road, Dorchester DT1 1RN. Telephone: Dorchester (0305) 64066.

The museum is housed in the formidable Victorian 'keep', more properly the gatehouse of the former Dorchester barracks. There are displays of uniform, equipment and other mementos of the campaigns covering five continents of the Dorset Regiment (Devonshire and Dorset Regiment since 1958), Dorset Militia and Volunteers, and Queen's Own Dorset Yeomanry. Among the exhibits is a gun captured from the French at Fort Marabout, Egypt, in 1802. There is also a reference library.

Tutankhamun Exhibition, 25 High West Street, Dorchester. Telephone: Dorchester (0305) 69571.

This is the only such exhibition outside Egypt, with facsimiles of the famous golden mask and other treasures from the boy king's tomb. The tomb and antechamber with their treasures are also recreated to show the magnificence of this great discovery.

GILLINGHAM

Gillingham Museum, Church Walk, Gillingham. Telephone: Gillingham (0747) 822173.

This small museum is crammed with material of local interest, including iron age and Romano-British archaeological finds, Gillingham brickmaking, charge boards of the Vale of Blackmoor Turnpike Trust, and a fire engine. There is a good collection of documents dating from the fourteenth century. One of the special exhibits is an elaborate wheelbarrow with a silver spade, used to cut the first sod when building the railway at Gillingham (opened 1859-60).

LANGTON MATRAVERS

Coach House Museum, St George's Close, Langton Matravers, Swanage. Telephone: Swanage (0929) 423168.

The museum is behind the church. It is a museum of the once important Purbeck stone and marble industries, with exhibits of masons' work from Roman times onwards. There are many photographs and items of quarrying and stone-dressing equipment.

LYME REGIS

Lyme Regis Museum, Bridge Street, Lyme Regis DT7 3QA. Telephone: Lyme Regis (029 74) 3370.

Lyme Regis is a fossil collecting centre of the Dorset coast, and there are some fine exhibits in the museum. These include the plesiosaur and ichthyosaur. Both types are associated with Mary Anning, a famous local fossiler who made spectacular finds in the early nineteenth century. Other fossils are on show, but there is also a section on the local history of Lyme Regis, with old paintings and photographs.

MILTON ABBAS

Park Farm Museum, Milton Abbas. Telephone: Milton Abbas (0258) 880216.

This is housed in former thatched carthorse stables. There is a comprehensive collection of Dorset farm implements and small items from the old Milton Abbas brewery, which closed in the 1950s. A pictorial history of the village includes old photographs and documents. Farm animals can be seen and fed nearby and there are pony and tractor rides in the summer holidays. The picnic site offers fine views towards Poole Harbour and the Isle of Wight.

OWERMOIGNE

Mill House Working Cider Museum, Owermoigne, Dorchester DT2 8HZ. Telephone: Dorchester (0305) 852220.

Many items of cider making from the West

Country are on display, including apple crushers and huge wooden screw-presses over two hundred years old. There is a video showing the process but this is a working museum and cider making with all its smells can be experienced in the autumn months.

POOLE

Guildhall Museum, Market Street, Poole BH15 1NP. Telephone: Poole (0202) 675151, extension 3550.

This fine Georgian market house of 1761 is on two floors, with outside steps leading to the upper. It was converted into public baths before it became a museum. Aspects of Poole's history are shown in a wide range of changing exhibitions.

The Old Lifeboat House, East Quay, Poole.

Located at the seaward end of Poole Quay, this historic lifeboat house contains the *Thomas Kirk Wright*, the port's lifeboat of 1938 and a veteran of the Dunkirk evacuation in 1940.

Royal National Lifeboat Museum, West Quay Road, Poole. Telephone: Poole (0202) 671133.

This is the museum of the lifeboat service at the Royal National Lifeboat Institution's headquarters. There is a comprehensive dis-

Guildhall Museum, Poole.

play of models, paintings, medals and photographs covering developments and notable events in the long history of the service. New exhibits are frequently introduced.

Scaplen's Court Museum, High Street, Poole. Telephone: Poole (0202) 675151, extension 3550.

In this notable fifteenth-century town house a variety of displays shows everyday life in Poole through the ages up to the eighteenth century. Domestic items are shown in reconstructed settings of a sitting room, kitchen and scullery. There is a central courtyard and walled garden.

Waterfront, 4 High Street, Poole. Telephone: Poole (0202) 675151, extension 3550.

This new museum incorporates five floors of a warehouse and the Town Cellars, a late fifteenth-century woolhouse and until recently the Maritime Museum. There is a reconstructed Victorian street scene, but most of the museum is devoted to the maritime history of Poole, such as crafts, trades and smuggling. Displays include an iron-age log boat dredged from the harbour, artefacts recovered from a wrecked Spanish vessel in Studland Bay and the remains of a medieval boat excavated at the nearby Poole Foundry site. The techniques of underwater archaeology are also explained.

PORTLAND

Chesil Gallery, Chiswell, Portland. Telephone: Portland (0305) 822738.

There are changing exhibitions of contemporary art by visiting sculptors and painters as well as those in residence. There is also an art bookshop in the gallery annexe.

Portland Museum, 217 Wakeham, Portland. Telephone: Portland (0305) 821804.

The museum premises include the attractive Avice's Cottage of 1640, given by Dr Marie Stopes, who founded the museum in 1930. This is one of the few seemingly sheltered spots on the island. The collection portrays the history of the island from early prehistoric times. There are two Roman stone coffins displayed behind the museum. Local history includes the stone industry and prison, as well as other aspects of island life. The maritime section has details of shipwrecks on the exposed Portland coast.

SHAFTESBURY

Shaftesbury Abbey and Museum, Park Walk, Shaftesbury. Telephone: Shaftesbury (0747) 52910.

King Alfred founded an abbey here in AD 880 for his daughter Ethelgiva. Edward the Martyr's bones were brought here from Wareham in AD 979, and it became a shrine for pilgrimage. By the Dissolution Shaftesbury had become the wealthiest Benedictine nunnery in England, with properties including the great tithe barn at Bradford-on-Avon, Wiltshire. The old abbey was a ready source of building stone in the town, so that only the foundations of the nave and east chapels can be seen in a garden setting. There is also the crypt of the Martyr's Chapel and a small museum with carvings and other relics.

Shaftesbury Local History Museum, Gold Hill, Shaftesbury. Telephone: Shaftesbury (0747) 52157.

Here is a well displayed museum, at the top of Gold Hill. Archaeological finds from Shaftesbury and surrounding parishes include a Roman child's coffin of lead, set in a stone tray, and remnants of the Shaftesbury hoard of Saxon silver pennies. As well as household items and agricultural tools there is a small collection of Dorset buttons of different styles. This was an important local industry until the 1850s. A curious exhibit is Shaftesbury's decorated Byzant, once used in an annual ceremony to ensure the right of the hilltop town to take water from Enmore Green below. Another is the dried cat from a cottage roof, where it was placed to scare away vermin.

SHERBORNE
Sherborne Museum, Abbey Gate House, Sherborne DT9 3BP. Telephone: Sherborne (093 581) 2252.

The museum lies between the abbey church and Cheap Street. Local history exhibits cover the abbey and Sherborne's two castles and their role in the Civil War. There are colour facsimiles of the very fine Sherborne Missal. Town photographs are of interest. Local industry is recognised in an exhibition about the former silk mill in the town, while a steam engine is displayed which once worked pumps for the Sherborne Gas and Coke Company.

STURMINSTER NEWTON
Sturminster Newton Museum, Bath Road, Sturminster Newton.

This museum opened in 1989 in the town's former workhouse chapel of the 1820s. Displays will change annually to show different aspects and periods of the district's history.

SWANAGE
The Tithe Barn Museum and Art Gallery, Church Hill, Swanage. Telephone: Swanage (0929) 424768.

There are natural history and geology sections, the latter including fossils and the oil industry. The most important local industry

The Martyrs' Tree and memorial seat, Tolpuddle.

around Swanage was the stone trade, and this has an important place in the museum. The art gallery stages an exhibition of local paintings of Swanage and its environs.

TOLPUDDLE
Tolpuddle Martyrs Memorial Museum, TUC Memorial Cottages, Tolpuddle.

This is a small and neat museum in the centre of the cottages erected as a memorial to the six famous martyrs who founded a union and were sentenced to seven years' transportation in 1834 for administering a secret oath. There are photographs and other old illustrations of agricultural workers, including the martyrs. When their sentences were repealed after a public outcry, five went on to Canada from Australia, and only James Hammett returned to Tolpuddle, in 1839. His grave is in the churchyard nearby. The old tree beneath which the men met is preserved in the village, which is on the busy A35.

WAREHAM

Wareham Town Museum, East Street, Wareham.

This museum is of special interest because of its collection of photographs and records of T. E. Lawrence (Lawrence of Arabia), who lived at Clouds Hill near Bovington. They trace his life from college days to the desert and his subsequent career to his death in 1935. Archaeological exhibits include a fine palaeolithic hand-axe, found in the river Frome, and copies of silver pennies minted at Wareham in the tenth century. There is a photographic record of old Wareham.

WEYMOUTH

Deep Sea Adventure and Shipwreck Centre, 9 Custom House Quay, Old Harbour, Weymouth. Telephone: Weymouth (0305) 760690.

The exciting story of diving is told with animated and interactive displays. Historic exhibits show Halley's diving bell and the diver who inspected the foundations of Winchester Cathedral. Difficult feats of salvage include diving to recover gold from the wartime wreck of HMS *Edinburgh*, while the *Titanic* display describes the sinking and subsequent discovery of this famous wreck using the very latest diving technology. There are many other interesting exhibits, and live diving displays in a special tank during the summer.

WIMBORNE MINSTER

Merley House and Model Museum, Merley, Wimborne. Telephone: Wimborne (0202) 886533.

The recently restored house dates from the 1750s and features some fine plaster ceilings. The model collection contains four thousand toy cars, ships and aeroplanes from the 1930s to the present, and includes many famous makers' products. Working N-gauge railway layouts are on display.

Priest's House Museum, 25 High Street, Wimborne Minster BH21 1HR. Telephone: Wimborne (0202) 882533.

The museum is housed in a Tudor building, with a garden. Exhibits cover archaeology and local history. Some iron age and Roman material is of note, including a Celtic tricephalos — a carved stone head with three faces.

Sturminster Newton watermill.

8
Other places to visit

Abbotsbury Swannery, Abbotsbury. Telephone: Abbotsbury (030 587) 228.

The Abbotsbury monks established this large and famous colony of mute swans in the fourteenth century. It is at the western end of the brackish waters of the Fleet, held back by the high bank of Chesil Beach. Eel grass is an important source of food for the swans. There are extensive reed beds — still used for thatch — and a mid seventeenth-century duck decoy.

Alderholt Mill, Alderholt, near Fordingbridge. Telephone: Fordingbridge (0425) 531130.

This restored watermill stands beside Ashford Water on the border with Hampshire. It has an art gallery and a shop selling locally made crafts and their stoneground flour.

Broadwindsor Craft Centre, Redlands Farm, Broadwindsor, near Beaminster. Telephone: Broadwindsor (0308) 68362.

The centre comprises shops selling local crafts with pottery and woodworking, and a museum of fossils, minerals, crystals and gemstone jewellery. There is a restaurant.

Butterfly Farm, Lodmoor Country Park, Weymouth. Telephone: Weymouth (0305) 783311.

Now one of the many attractions at the Lodmoor Country Park, the Butterfly Farm has a large jungle flight area, caterpillar breeding centre and insect house.

Corfe Castle Model Village, The Square, Corfe Castle. Telephone: Corfe Castle (0929) 481234.

An attractive garden is the perfect setting for a model of a village such as Corfe. The castle has been re-created to show how it looked in its original state.

Dinosaurland, Coombe Street, Lyme Regis. Telephone: Lyme Regis (02974) 3541.

A gallery walk through geological time puts into context the Jurassic period of 195 million years ago. This is the age from which most of the local fossils on display have come, from ammonites to the bones of the icthyosaur and plesiosaur. There are also life-size exhibits, a video showing the winter world of fossil hunters, a fossil and dinosaur shop and guided beach walks.

The Dorset Heavy Horse Centre, Brambles Farm, Edmondsham, Verwood BH21 5RJ. Telephone: Verwood (0202) 824040.

The centre is about a mile north of Verwood. It is a purpose-built showplace and a must for enthusiasts. The famous Maniton Shire horse team is based here, and there are also Percheron, Clydesdale and Suffolk heavy horses. They can be seen in their stables, in harness and working, or on parade. Horse-drawn farm machinery and equipment are also on view.

Dorset Rare Breeds Centre and Farm Museum, Shaftesbury Road, Gillingham. Telephone: Gillingham (0747) 822169.

Rare and endangered breeds of sheep, cattle and pigs can be seen in the enclosures, while the popular children's corner has goats and hens. The museum contains a selection of horse-drawn vehicles and farm implements. There is also a demonstration milking unit.

Glen's Bird Farm, Woolgarston Farm, Corfe Castle. Telephone: Corfe Castle (0929) 480521.

Over sixty species of exotic birds are displayed in landscaped gardens to the east of Corfe Castle, with views of the Purbeck hills. Some of the birds are fond of human company and a blue-fronted Amazon parrot has a vocabulary large enough even to recite poems.

The Great Shire Horse Centre, Lodmoor Country Park, Weymouth. Telephone: Weymouth (0305) 775315.

This is the home of the Devenish Brewery Shires, which can be seen in their stables or on parade and drawing wagons for rides. There are demonstrations of grooming, plaiting and harnessing, and displays of drays, farm wagons and agricultural machinery.

Lodmoor Country Park, Weymouth. Telephone: Weymouth (0305) 777696 (season only).

This 350 acre (142 ha) site is close to the shore and Weymouth's sea front. The main attractions are the **Sea Life Centre**, **Butterfly Farm**, **Model World** and **Great Shire Horse Centre** (see individual entries), while other leisure facilities include mini-golf and a miniature railway. The sea-marsh lake of the Lodmoor Nature Reserve (RSPB) is accessible by path, and there are display boards and a hide.

Melbury Abbas Mill, Melbury Abbas, Shaftesbury. Telephone: Shaftesbury (0747) 52163.

A mill in working order forms part of a farm complex beside the river Sturkel, a tributary of the Stour. A large millpond supplies the water for an iron overshot wheel, 11 feet (3.3 m) in diameter and 6 feet (1.8 m) wide. It was made at Bourton in 1875. Various tools and milling equipment are displayed inside. There were once at least five mills within a short stretch of the river. Another survives just downstream at Cann Mill, which produces wholemeal flour commercially. The Mediterranean-style windmill on the roof is a curious feature.

Merley Bird Gardens, Merley, Wimborne. Telephone: Wimborne (0202) 883790.

Many exotic birds are on view in a large walled garden of the eighteenth-century Merley House. There are formal gardens, water gardens and shrubberies. In contrast to the more colourful jungle birds, there is a large collection of penguins.

Model World, Lodmoor Country Park, Weymouth. Telephone: Weymouth (0305) 781797.

Hundreds of hand-made models can be seen in model towns and villages, with a railway, zoo, airport, fair and space centre, all set in an attractive garden.

Monkey World, Longthorns, near Bovington. Telephone: Bindon Abbey (0929) 462537.

Woodland walks enable visitors to see a variety of animals in a more natural environment than a conventional zoo. Primates here range from Barbary apes to ring-tailed lemurs. This is also a chimpanzee rescue centre for animals recovered from grim lives as photographic 'models' on Spanish beaches.

Moors Valley Country Park, Horton Road, Ashley Heath, near Ringwood. Telephone: Ringwood (0425) 470721.

A central attraction is the lakeside Moors Valley Railway, a narrow-gauge steam railway, but there are also lakeside and forest walks, picnic areas, an adventure playground, a nine-hole golf course and a restaurant in a sixteenth-century barn.

The Natural World, Poole Quay, Poole. Telephone: Poole (0202) 686712.

The complex incorporates Poole Aquarium and Serpentarium. Creatures which both fascinate and horrify include sharks, piranhas, deadly snakes, caimans, alligators, crocodiles, spiders, scorpions and insects. In the snake pit, visitors can meet a snake face to face.

Poole Pottery, Poole Quay, Poole. Telephone: Poole (0202) 666200.

This famous factory has a large craft showroom displaying the great range of pottery products made here. A special exhibition shows the history of pottery-making with displays, models and videos, including a reconstructed Purbeck clay mine and bottle kiln.

The Rare Poultry, Pig and Plant Centre, Long Ash Farm, near Milton Abbas DT11 0BX. Telephone: Milton Abbas (0258) 880447.

The centre is about 1 mile (1.6 km) south-west of Milton Abbas and has over sixty breeds of poultry displayed in enclosures, including the very rare Marsh Daisy and Legbar breeds. All rare British pig breeds are here too.

Sea Life Centre, Lodmoor Country Park, Weymouth DT4 7SX. Telephone: Weymouth (0305) 760674.

This well laid-out centre covers different themes and gives visitors the experience of viewing hundreds of curious sea creatures at eye level. These include catfish, conger eels, stingrays, trigger fish and tropical sharks. Living 'touch' pools allow the close observation of creatures from the British coastline, and there are also a children's Blue Whale Splashpool, mini submarine and picnic area.

Sturminster Newton Mill, Sturminster Newton. Telephone: Sturminster Newton (0258) 72275 or 73151.

There has been a mill here, in a picturesque setting at a weir on the Stour, since at least Domesday times. It is probable that Glastonbury Abbey owned this and Fiddleford Mill just downstream. The present building is L-shaped, the stone part dating from the seventeenth century, with the brick extension about a hundred years later. Twin undershot wheels were replaced by a more efficient turbine (by Armfields of Ringwood) in 1904, and this is still the driving power. The mill was restored in 1981 and is open to the public, who can watch all the processes, from the delivery of grain through to finished flour and animal feeds. There is a small picnic site behind the mill.

Swanage Railway, The Station, Swanage BH19 1HB. Telephone: Swanage (0929) 425800.

The branch line from Wareham to Swanage carried passengers from 1885 until 1972. Despite views that it was a valuable asset, the lines were lifted between Swanage and Furzebrook, where sidings serve the clay and oil industries. Now restoration is under way, and steam trains run to Harman's Cross from Swanage station (fortunately saved from demolition). The workshops may be viewed here. Rolling stock includes the Brighton Belle's Pullman car number 88, a Class 25 diesel electric locomotive and a Stanier 8F steam locomotive brought back in 1989 from Turkey, where it had worked for 48 years. Of local interest is a locomotive used by Mowlem and Company when building the King George V graving dock at Southampton in 1933. The firm's founder, John Mowlem, was born in Swanage (see chapter 10).

Worldwide Butterflies and Lullingstone Silk Farm, Compton House, Over Compton, Sherborne. Telephone: Yeovil (0935) 74608.

This is between Sherborne and Yeovil, off the A30. Within the historic Compton House are live butterflies in exotic settings with tropical plants. A collection of worldwide specimens is displayed in the library. Here also is the Lullingstone Silk Farm — the only one in Britain — where silk worms are reared and silk is reeled. Outside, there are pleasant walks through the Butterfly Gardens, where plants have been chosen to attract many species. In the special butterfly house visitors can walk among the butterflies.

Upwey Wishing Well, Church Street, Upwey, near Weymouth. Telephone: Upwey (030 581) 2262.

This is said to be the greatest natural spring in Britain, where visitors can wish at the famous well in an attractive water garden. There are a gift shop and café.

Walford Mill Craft Centre, Knobcrook Road, Wimborne. Telephone: Wimborne (0202) 841400.

The Dorset Craft Guild occupies this large brick mill building beside the Allen river. There are shops, a gallery and a restaurant.

The Watermill at Upwey, Church Street, Upwey, near Weymouth DT3 5QE. Telephone: Upwey (0305) 814233.

This tall stone-built mill dates from 1802, with a huge waterwheel 22 feet (6.7 m) in diameter and 9 feet (2.7 m) wide. Visitors can see the two pairs of stones producing flour, which is for sale.

Hardy's Cottage, Higher Bockhampton.

9
Thomas Hardy's Dorset

Thomas Hardy (1840-1928) is Dorset's best known novelist and poet. The scene of events in his novels is mostly Dorset, with surrounding counties from time to time, and it was in this region that he created his 'Wessex'. Frequently he substituted his own names for existing placenames; sometimes his names are clearly fictitious. Hardy is celebrated for his descriptions of the rural scene of nineteenth-century Dorset, as yet hardly affected by the modern age. Much pleasure can be gained by unravelling the landscape from his descriptions and placenames. Following this up takes one into some of the finer parts of the countryside. Of all his novels *Tess of the d'Urbervilles* paints the broadest canvas, as Tess's journeys took her across much of the county. Several of the places featured in the book form the basis of this small selection of Hardy's Dorset.

Bere Regis

This was 'Kingsbere', where Tess mused over the d'Urberville (Turberville) tombs and crypt in the church, when her family fortunes had reached their lowest and they were camping under the window outside. The Turbervilles were a once important local family, from which Hardy adapted the name.

Blackmoor Vale

Tess was brought up here in the 'Vale of Little Dairies', bounded on the south by high chalk hills. The vale is still important for dairying, with small fields and tree-lined hedges. From a distance, the vale is little changed from Hardy's descriptions. Common usage has the spelling as Blackmore, while the Ordnance Survey prefers Blackmoor.

Cranborne

The little market town of 'Chaseborough' features in the early part of *Tess of the d'Urbervilles*. The 'Flower-de-Luce' inn is clearly the Fleur de Lys, on the corner opposite the church. Nearby Pentridge ('Trantridge') has less to offer, and the d'Urberville mansion of 'The Slopes' is complete fiction.

Cross-in-Hand, Batcombe.

This is difficult to find, on the north side of the ridge road from Holywell to Dogbury Gate, just west of the turning to Hilfield (OS 194; ST631038). It is part of an old stone pillar, upon which Tess was obliged to place her hand and swear never again to tempt Alex d'Urberville. It is a lovely spot, with fine views over the 'Vale of Little Dairies' (Blackmoor Vale).

Dorchester

This is Hardy's 'Casterbridge', with many associations. He was born within 3 miles (5 km) and finally came to live here at Max Gate, the house he had built in 1885. It is now a private residence, but his study has been faithfully reconstructed in the County Museum. Here one can see his desks, writing equipment, books and manuscripts. There are further mementos in the main hall of the museum. These include some of Hardy's original watercolours and a map of Wessex with his placenames marked. The County Reference Library at Colliton Park has another important collection of manuscripts. Nearby, the seated figure of Hardy looks out on to a busy roundabout at Top o' Town. This bronze sculpture on its Portland stone base is the work of Eric Kennington. Dorchester is described in *The Mayor of Casterbridge*. A plaque records that the brick-built Barclay's Bank in South Street is the reputed home of Hardy's mayor. The Roman amphitheatre of Maumbury Rings was the scene in the book for the encounter between Michael Henchard and his long-lost wife. The special Thomas Hardy's Ale, the strongest beer in Britain, is brewed in Dorchester, keeping close to Hardy's description in *The Trumpet-Major*.

'Egdon Heath', near Higher Bockhampton.

This is Hardy's name for the great area of heathland which once covered a large part of Dorset, eastwards from Dorchester. Much has since been reclaimed or forested, so it is now very fragmented. Puddletown Heath, behind Hardy's birthplace, is now mostly forested. This is an area he must have known well, and he describes it in *The Return of the Native*. Rainbarrow (which features in the novel) and Duddle Heath are accessible by footpath from Higher Bockhampton.

Evershot

This village is Hardy's 'Evershed'. The Acorn Inn at the top of the main street is named the Sow-and-Acorn in *Tess*. She passed here on her walk to visit Angel Clare's parents at Beaminster ('Emminster'). She rested and fed at a nearby cottage, which may be the Tess Cottage by the church, although this is named after another Tess. The village of Evershot is worth a visit.

'Flintcomb-Ash', near Plush.

This is the windswept chalk table land where the abandoned Tess spent a cruel winter of open-air work. The exact location of this 'starve-acre' farm is unclear, although most likely it is the area round Nettlecombe Tout or Church Hill, just north of the tiny hamlet of Plush (OS 194; ST 714021). Dole's Ash Farm, about a mile east of Piddletrenthide, is also

possible, although this is about 300 feet (91 m) below the high chalk plateau.

Frome Valley, from West Stafford to Wool.

This is the 'Vale of the Great Dairies', where Tess worked as a milkmaid at 'Talbothays Dairy'. There is no one recognisable site, although the West Stafford area is more likely, as Hardy's father had a farm here of that name. However, the 'verdant plain so well watered by the river Var or Froom' is still important for dairying. Its lush meadows with traces of irrigation channels are in remarkable contrast to the heathlands on either side. The settlements keep to higher ground, but the river can be reached at Moreton and Woodsford.

Hardy's Cottage, Higher Bockhampton, Dorchester. Telephone: Dorchester (0305) 62366. National Trust.

Thomas Hardy was born here, about 2½ miles (4 km) north-east of Dorchester, in 1840. The cottage was built by his great grandfather in 1801 and is an idyllic thatched country cottage with a charming garden at the front. Behind the cottage is a granite stone erected in 1932 by American admirers. This is the last house in the hamlet, before the forest closes in. Beyond are remnants of the 'Egdon Heath' which Hardy loved so much. The best approach to the cottage is through the woodland path from the car park.

Marnhull

Tess's 'Marlott', where she was born and lived her early life, Marnhull is a large village today, with no real centre. Near the church, the Crown Inn was the 'Pure Drop Inn' of *Tess*. Today it has an appropriately named bar. The so-called Tess Cottage at Walton Elm may not be the home envisaged by Hardy.

Piddletrenthide church

The church is a short distance north of the main village. A small notice in the churchyard points out two early seventeenth-century headstones, to William and Thomas Dumberfield, a family immortalised by Thomas Hardy's Tess Durbeyfield. The church (All Saints) has carved figures on the tower and buttresses, and a small Norman south door.

Portland, the 'Isle of Slingers'

This was the scene for *The Well-Beloved*. Such was the quarrying activity in Hardy's time that he likened the many derrick cranes to a 'swarm of crane-flies' crouched on the summit plateau. Avice's Cottage, home of Avice Caro, is now part of the island's museum. At an earlier period, Anne Loveday watched from Portland Bill as the English fleet passed down the Channel (*The Trumpet-Major*).

Haycocks above the river Stour.

Poxwell manor house

Beside the A353 is an early seventeenth-century manor house with a walled garden and small gatehouse. Hardy chose this for the 'Oxwell Hall' of Squire Derriman in *The Trumpet-Major*.

Puddletown

Puddletown is the 'Weatherbury' of *Far from the Madding Crowd*. Just up the valley, Hardy used Waterston Manor as the basis for Bathsheba Everdene's 'Weatherbury Farm', and Druce Farm for Farmer Boldwood's 'Little Weatherbury'. Water from a gargoyle on the church tower washed away the flowers on poor Fanny Robin's grave beneath.

Shaftesbury

Hardy used the old word 'Shaston' for this 'mountain town', which has a significant place in *Jude the Obscure*. Gillingham also features but retains its true name. It was from hilltop 'Shaston' that Jack Durbeyfield was descending at the opening of *Tess*.

Stinsford church

This is near Hardy's birthplace, 1¼ miles (2 km) east of Dorchester. Hardy's heart is buried beside his first wife, Emma, who died in 1912. His ashes are in Westminster Abbey. Stinsford appears as 'Mellstock' in many of his works.

Sturminster Newton.

This is Hardy's 'Stourcastle'. With Emma, he rented 'Riverside' in 1876-8. The house overlooks an island in the Stour to the west of the town. Here he wrote *The Return of the Native*.

Sutton Poyntz

Loveday's mill was at 'Overcombe' in the *The Trumpet-Major*. It may be Sutton Poyntz, which nestles below the chalk downs, 3 miles (5 km) north-east of Weymouth. Hardy may also have used elements of Bincombe, just to the west. In the book, the soldiers camped and paraded on the downs hereabouts.

Weymouth

Hardy's 'Budmouth' appears frequently in his writings. In *The Trumpet-Major*, he describes the town and surrounding district at the period in the Napoleonic Wars when invasion seemed imminent.

Woolbridge Manor, Wool

This is 'Wellbridge', the Elizabethan manor where Tess and Angel Clare spent their ill-fated wedding night. It is a solid building with tall chimneys and stands near the old bridge across the Frome. It is now thankfully bypassed and left in peace, just north of the village. The ruined Bindon Abbey also features in this sorry episode of *Tess of the d'Urbervilles*.

The Great Barn, Abbotsbury.

10
Towns and villages

ABBOTSBURY

This is a pretty village of local stone with thatch, but the road through the centre can be busy in the summer. The site is sheltered, about a mile inland from Chesil Beach, tucked in under a high hill which has signs of medieval field systems. The church (St Nicholas) is mostly fifteenth-century but is made rather townish within by the additions of later centuries. The pulpit bears scars of the Civil War. The effigy of an abbot in the north porch is a reminder of the former Benedictine abbey. Inside, a good drawing shows how it may have looked. At the Dissolution in 1539 the abbey and much of the village were granted to Sir Giles Strangways, in whose family they still remain.

There are some traces of the abbey to the south of the church, including a gateway arch, but Abbotsbury's great treasure is the thatched tithe barn beside the village pond. The Great Barn is 272 feet (83 m) long and is impressive, even though half is roofless. It is kept locked, as thatching reeds cut from the Fleet are stored inside, but the buttressed stone walls can be examined in the ruined part. On an isolated hill stands the fourteenth-century St Catherine's Chapel. It is heavily built, with a barrel-vaulted roof. This fine structure makes a distinctive landmark and is in the care of English Heritage. The old monastic Swannery and the later Sub-Tropical Gardens are probably the most popular attractions at Abbotsbury (chapters 5 and 8).

ASHMORE

This is the highest village in Dorset, at 700 feet (213 m) on top of the chalk downs on the edge of Cranborne Chase, 5 miles (8 km) south-east of Shaftesbury. Flint and stone houses, both large and humble, cluster around a large round duck pond. The pond, and therefore this farming community, may date back to Romano-British times. Houses and farms follow the three lanes which radiate from the central pond. Manor Farm has some stonework believed to have come from Eastbury House at Tarrant Gunville, demolished around 1780. Beside the farm, the church (St Nicholas) is mainly of 1874.

BEAMINSTER

Early closing Wednesday.

This small neat town lies near the source of the river Brit and sits in a bowl of farmed and wooded hills. It is a town of brown stone and worth a quiet investigation. The Market Place forms the centre, where there are seventeenth- and eighteenth-century houses, most with interesting features. A lane leads down to the large parish church (St Mary), which has a tall sixteenth-century tower of Ham stone and features carved figures. Restoration of the mid nineteenth century has left a disappointing interior. There are monuments to the Strode family of Parnham. The nearby almshouses are also associated with the Strodes. Parnham House is just south of the town, beside the river Brit, and Mapperton is to the east

51

(chapter 5). The small and interesting village of Broadwindsor, 3 miles (5 km) to the west, has a craft centre (see chapter 8).

BERE REGIS

This village has long since lost the importance it had in medieval times, when there were close associations with royalty. More recently it was at a major road junction, with heavy traffic in the narrow streets, but peace has returned with a new bypass. The main street has cottages which mostly date from after a fire of 1788, but the church (St John the Baptist) is the main point of interest in the village (chapter 6). It has associations with Thomas Hardy's *Tess of the d'Urbervilles* (chapter 9). To the east, the village is overlooked by the hillfort on Woodbury Hill, the site of fairs from at least the thirteenth century. This was the 'Greenhill Fair' in Hardy's *Far from the Madding Crowd*. Just to the west, the hamlet of Shitterton has attractive thatched cottages.

BLANDFORD FORUM

Early closing Wednesday.

Despite its name, this was never a Roman town. It lies on the north side of the river Stour, at an important crossing point. A disastrous fire broke out in 1731, which destroyed much of the town and two adjacent villages, taking seventy-four lives. The town was rebuilt, mostly in brick of different shades, giving a pleasing appearance. John and William Bastard were the architects responsible for the rebuilding and there are many good examples of Georgian architecture. On the south side of the Market Place there are fine brick buildings above the shops. Of note is the decoration above the entrance to the Red Lion yard. The north side is conspicuous for the Corn Exchange (Town Hall of 1734), built in Portland stone and entered beneath tall arches. Here is also the church (St Peter and St Paul), in greensand and Portland stone. The 80 foot (24 m) tower and cupola dominate the town. The church was completed in 1739 and is a fine period piece. Inside are box pews and a gallery, and huge rounded pillars support the roof of the nave. The ceilings are decorated, especially in the apse at the east end. Boards on the walls list details of benefactions to the needy of the town.

Outside the church is a small Doric portico of 1760, which once housed a pump. This was erected 'in remembrance of God's dreadful visitation by fire' by John Bastard, 'a considerable sharer in the general calamity'. Almost opposite is the museum in Bere's Yard (chapter 7). It is worth exploring other streets, including the delightfully named The Plocks. The Close contains Old House (about 1660), which survived the fire. This is an extravagan-

za in brick, with two huge chimneys. In Salisbury Street, George Ryve's almshouses of 1682 are also survivors. In West Street, note the milestone, 104 miles to Hyde Park Corner.

Over the bridge is Blandford St Mary and the 'Badger' brewery of Hall and Woodhouse, a firm established in 1777. Across the meadows beside the Stour is the brick and stone Bryanston House, now a public school. It was the last great country house to be built in Dorset, being completed in 1890 by the Portmans. A new ring road has greatly relieved congestion in the town. The Great Dorset Steam Fair is held annually in late summer at Tarrant Hinton, 2 miles (3.2 km) to the north-east.

BOURNEMOUTH

Early closing Wednesday.

Bournemouth's popularity as a resort is justly deserved — the climate is mild and there are good beaches of golden sand and the piers. Until 1974 Bournemouth was part of Hamp-

This elaborate memorial to the great fire of Blandford Forum was erected by John Bastard in 1760.

Modern Bournemouth is in stark contrast to much of Dorset.

shire. Now the whole conurbation from Poole to Christchurch lies within Dorset. The first house was erected in 1810 by Lewis Tregonwell, in a peaceful valley where a stream entered the sea. The popularity of the area has grown rapidly since, with developments westwards into Westbourne, where trees are as much a feature as hotels and large villas. There are also steep wooded valleys (chines) leading down to the sea. To the east are the suburbs of Boscombe and Southbourne. A valley road descends to Boscombe Pier, and undercliff promenades lie behind the beach in both directions. On the top of the sandy cliff, it is fortunate that development did not reach the edge. Overcliff drives give access to fine views of Christchurch Bay, towards Old Harry Rocks and Swanage in one direction, and the Isle of Wight in the other.

The centre of Bournemouth holds the greatest architectural interest. Here gardens have been laid out on both sides of the stream in the valley bottom, emerging at Bournemouth Pier with its theatre. The Royal Exeter Hotel in Exeter Road is the site of Tregonwell's original house, but this is now lost amidst more recent development. Clustered in this area, places of entertainment include the Pavilion and the Winter Gardens (home of the Bournemouth Symphony Orchestra). The new Bournemouth International Centre dominates the scene on the west side.

Two Victorian churches are of interest. The brick and stone Town Hall is disappointing architecturally, but this is compensated for by the nearby St Stephens Church in St Stephens Road. It has a square-topped west tower and was designed by J. L. Pearson, whose other works included Truro Cathedral. Inside it is dark and spacious, with a seeming forest of pillars, but a haven of peace from the bustle of the town outside. The parish church of St Peter, at the corner of Hinton Road, has a tall tower and spire, 202 feet (61 m) high. Inside it has a long nave. John Keble, an important figure in the Anglican church, worshipped here after his retirement to Bournemouth in 1865, and his chapel is on the south side. A plaque in the choir stalls records that Gladstone made his last communion in the church, on 13th March 1898. Straddling a path in the churchyard is the tomb of Lewis Tregonwell, founder of Bournemouth, and other family members. There is also the white marble tomb of Mary Shelley. See chapter 7 for Bournemouth's museums.

BRIDPORT
Early closing Thursday, market days Wednesday and Saturday.

An interesting town, Bridport has long been associated with rope and net making. Locally grown flax was the basis of this industry, which is still carried on by Bridport-Gundry Limited, off West Street. This firm's origins date back to 1665, when Samuel Gundry established his first net works. The main street, actually West and East Streets, easily accommodates the traffic of the A35 because of its great width. South Street is also wide, because fishing nets were made there in times past. Narrow alleyways leading off at right angles were once ropewalks.

The three principal streets all have good examples of Georgian buildings, often in brick. On the corner where they meet, the Town Hall of 1785 is of note. Its large clock tower was added later. Across the road, a sign over Beach and Company's bow-windowed pharmacy records that this was the George Inn, which Charles II visited in September 1651, while fleeing after the battle of Worcester. Still in East Street are the classical Unitarian Chapel (1794) and the Literary and Scientific Institute (1834), now the library. In South Street are the museum, in an early sixteenth-century stone building (chapter 7), and the parish church of St Mary. The latter is less interesting within than its brown stone exterior suggests. In the southern part of the town is Palmer's small brewery, which serves the local area.

West Bay, now a small holiday resort, was the former port for Bridport, where raw materials for rope and net making were brought in. Shipbuilding also took place here. The narrow harbour entrance is at right angles to the coast, to keep it clear of shingle, but it funnels huge waves when seas are rough. To the east, the shingle beach is the beginning of Chesil Beach and is backed by the vertical East Cliff of yellowish Bridport sands. Westwards are tall crumbling cliffs and Eype Mouth and Seatown, where two valleys meet the sea.

BURTON BRADSTOCK

For somewhere so close to coastal tourist developments, this is a surprisingly pretty village of local yellow stone. It has been saved by being set back from the mouth of the Bride, which runs parallel to the coast for a while. The church (St Mary) is of the fourteenth century, with a south aisle of 1897, but is disappointing inside. The village is the gateway to the picturesque Bride valley, with its settlements of Litton Cheney, Long Bredy and Littlebredy.

CATTISTOCK

This small village is enhanced by winding streets and houses of stone, brick and flint. The church (St Peter and St Paul) was rebuilt in 1857 by Sir George Gilbert Scott, but the additions made by his son in 1874 are of special note. These include the north aisle, porch and tower. The last is the glory of the church: tall, with corner pinnacles and long bell openings. The decoration within is also fine. The village is deep in the Frome valley.

CERNE ABBAS

Almost lost in the deep Cerne valley, Cerne Abbas was once an important place but was passed by in the railway age. Probably better known for its chalk-cut Giant (chapter 3) and

former abbey, this is a pleasant village to wander around, with houses mainly of flint and brick, but some stone. The Benedictine abbey was founded in about AD 987 on the site of an earlier monastery on the north side of the village. Abbey Street leads to the few remaining fragments of the abbey and the Giant's Hill. At its end, the present churchyard is the site of the abbey church. St Augustine's Well is here, sheltered beneath trees. All that remains of the abbey is the ornate porch of the Abbots Hall, with a fine oriel window and fan vaulting. It was built by Abbot Thomas Sam (1497-1509). The fifteenth-century Guest House is a simpler building, with a small oriel window. The mid fourteenth-century tithe barn is partly converted to a house in the south-west part of the village.

The church (St Mary) has a tall tower of brown Ham stone. Inside there is much light because of plain glass windows. Important features include the stone chancel screen, fourteenth-century wall paintings in the chancel and a Jacobean pulpit. Note also the small heraldic glass in the fifteenth-century east window, which may have come from the abbey. Opposite the church, in Abbey Street, is a superb timbered building with stone footings known as the Pitchmarket.

The church tower dominates Abbey Street in Cerne Abbas.

The Constable's House is a fine Norman building beside the millstream at Christchurch.

CHARMOUTH

In a sense, Charmouth is a smaller version of neighbouring Lyme Regis, with Regency and early Victorian villas which give it the flavour of a resort of the pre-railway age. It was developed a short distance inland from the sea, around an earlier settlement. The main street climbs steeply up the west side of the Char valley but is, alas, the main A35. The Queen's Arms has early Tudor origins. Catharine of Aragon stayed here in 1501, and it was also where Charles II was to have made a rendezvous with the local captain Stephen Limbry, who had agreed to take the fugitive to France in 1651. The church (St Andrew) was rebuilt in the 1830s, when the resort was still expanding. A fossil exhibition with shop is also of note here. The sandy beach is at the mouth of the Char, where small boats are launched. This is a good place for fossil collecting, where fossils are washed out on to the beach from the slumping cliffs of Black Ven and Stonebarrow on either side. Visitors are warned that these cliffs are highly dangerous and constantly on the move.

CHIDEOCK

Between Bridport and Charmouth, the busy A35 descends steeply from both directions and runs through this attractive village with its cottages of local golden stone and thatch. The church (St Giles) is mainly of the fifteenth century but was restored in 1884. Among the monuments is the black marble tomb of Sir John Arundel (1575). Just north of the village, some earthworks of a fifteenth-century castle can be traced. To the south, a lane leads to Seatown, where there is an inn and a few houses at the mouth of the river Winniford. Access can be gained to the shore, and there are exhilarating clifftop walks to the west (Golden Cap) and east.

CHRISTCHURCH

Early closing Wednesday.

Christchurch stands at the meeting of the Avon and Stour rivers, at the head of Christchurch Harbour. It was known as Twyneham in Saxon times but owes its present name to the magnificent priory church. This church of the long-demolished priory is noted for its fine architecture and great length (chapter 6). The ruined keep of the Norman castle stands on a mound to the north. Nearby is the shell of the Constable's House, which is a good example of domestic Norman architecture (chapter 4). At the end of Castle Street, the sixteenth-century Town Bridge crosses the Avon.

Brick buildings in the attractive High Street and Church Street have the feel of Hampshire, to which the town belonged until 1974. The Old Town Hall has a cupola and an arched ground floor, giving access to a shopping precinct behind. It dates from the mid eighteenth century, when it was erected at the corner of Castle and Church Streets, only to be later moved to its present site in the High Street. The Quay provides a popular place

55

from which to hire boats or enjoy the view of the harbour. Here, Place Mill belonged to the priory before the Dissolution in 1539. It continued working until early in the twentieth century. Since restored, it is open to the public in the summer. A landscaped walk follows the millstream back to the Town Bridge. Christchurch's two museums are in this area (chapter 7).

In the Priory Gardens is the unusual mausoleum of a Mrs Perkins, who had a horror of being buried alive. She died in 1783, and her coffin had a lock which could be opened from the inside, in case she revived. The mausoleum was erected near the boys' school, so she could be heard. Her body was removed when her husband died in 1803, and the mausoleum was re-erected in its present position.

CORFE CASTLE

Corfe was the centre of the Purbeck marble industry in the middle ages, and the Ancient Society of Purbeck Marblers and Stone Cutters still meets here on Shrove Tuesdays. This attractive village suffers from the busy A351 from Wareham to Swanage, although West Street is quieter. The castle (chapter 4) towers over the scene. The village is of interest, too, with most houses having Purbeck stone walls and roofs. In the Market Place, the Greyhound Hotel with its porch is well placed for travellers on the main road. The church (St Edward) was rebuilt in the mid nineteenth century, and its large interior is rather plain. However, the earlier tower has superb gargoyles, a credit to the local stone masons. Just below in West Street, the minute Town Hall has a museum (chapter 7). Another attraction at Corfe Castle is a scale model of the village and castle (chapter 8).

CRANBORNE

This small village with its mainly brick houses has an air which suggests former importance. Indeed, a market was once held here. It lies in the north-east corner of Cranborne Chase, where the chalklands give way to the sands and clays of the Hampshire Basin. Here is the early seventeenth-century Manor House, built by the first Earl of Salisbury around an earlier hunting lodge used by King John. The walled gardens are occasionally open to the public (chapter 5). The church is described in chapter 6. Edmondsham House is 1 mile (1.6 km) to the south-east (chapter 5).

DORCHESTER

Early closing Thursday, market day Wednesday.

This is Dorset's bustling county town, small enough to appreciate. Dorchester is an impor-

tant route centre, and from a distance its outline is dominated by its churches, the Keep and the red-bricked Victorian prison. It was the *Durnovaria* of the Romans, and the course of the town wall can be followed on two sides by the 'Walks'. The South, Bowling Alley and West Walks are lined with avenues of trees and provide luxurious pedestrian ways while giving an indication of the size of the Roman town. Behind the uninspiring County Hall are the remains of a fourth-century town house, with a mosaic, well and hypocausts. The Roman amphitheatre of Maumbury Rings is at Weymouth Avenue in the southern part of the town. Public executions took place here up to the eighteenth century.

Of Dorchester's churches, it is worth finding St George's, an island of stone surrounded by brick houses and the green in the quiet suburb of Fordington. This long church may have been the first in England to be dedicated to St George. There is an exceptionally fine Norman tympanum over the south door, depicting St George aiding the Crusaders at the Battle of Antioch. Inside, Norman pillars have curious bases, the result of lowering the church floor. One incorporates a Roman capital, and there may have been a Roman building here. St Peter's church (High West Street) is townish inside, although there are effigies of knights

St Peter's church, Dorchester.

and some good later monuments. Outside, carved animals are of note.

Dorchester featured in the events following the Monmouth Rebellion of 1685. Lord Chief Justice Jeffreys held his Bloody Assizes in the Oak Room of the Antelope Hotel in South Street. Several hundred rebels were sentenced to death or transportation for life, and some were hung, drawn and quartered in the street outside. Nearby is the Town Pump, an obelisk erected in 1784 on the site of the old market house. Out of place in this busy shopping street is the Napper's Mite, a stone almshouse with a central courtyard. It was built in 1610 by Sir John Napier for ten poor men but now incorporates shops and a restaurant.

Another restaurant and teashop is Judge Jeffreys' Lodgings in High West Street. This is a superb timbered building of the early seventeenth century, and it is where the judge is believed to have stayed during his brief but terrible visit to the town. Across the road are the offices of West Dorset District Council and the Old Crown Court, where the Tolpuddle Martyrs were sentenced in 1834. In the same street are the Victorian-built County Museum and Town Hall, with its corner clock and spire. The two churches are St Peter's and All Saints', the latter now disused but distinguished by its tall spire.

Although fires have destroyed many earlier buildings, there is confident Georgian and Victorian domestic architecture. These are mainly of brick and include villas and humbler terraces, all found by exploring the back streets within a short distance of the central shopping streets.

Among industrial buildings, the Dorchester Brewery of 1880 presents a fine decorated red and cream brick facade to Weymouth Avenue. This is owned by Eldridge Pope and Company Limited, and visits can be arranged. There is also a small brewery museum.

Two famous Dorset poets are commemorated in the town. There is a statue of William Barnes outside St Peter's church, and one of Thomas Hardy at the roundabout at Top o' Town. There are also important Hardy collections in the County Reference Library and County Museum. Other museums are the Dinosaur Museum in Icen Way, and the Dorset Military Museum in the imposing Keep in Bridport Road. See chapter 7 for the museums and chapter 3 for Roman Dorchester.

GILLINGHAM
Early closing Thursday.

A small town in north Dorset, with a railway station on the Exeter-Waterloo line, Gillingham lacks any coherent architectural style, but a few interesting buildings can be found, in stone or locally made brick. The old Town Mill

in the centre is burnt out. The church (St Mary) was mainly rebuilt in 1838-40. The outside is pleasing, in pale limestone, while the interior is rather plain. In the north chapel is a large marble monument to Mrs Frances Dirdoe, who died in 1733, aged thirty-four. Behind the organ are the effigies of Thomas and John Jesop, a vicar and physician, dated 1625. Both appear to be holding hands. Steps lead into the south chapel, which is dedicated to the memory of a son of the Cross family, killed in action in the closing stages of the First World War. The town museum is in a row of cottages opposite the church (chapter 7).

LYME REGIS
Early closing Thursday.

Steep hills descend to this resort, which is almost on the Devon border and looks out over the wide sweep of Lyme Bay to Portland. The town was granted a charter in 1284 by Edward I, hence the 'Regis'. Later historical events concern the Civil War and the Monmouth Rebellion. The town has been a small resort since the eighteenth century. The Cobb is a breakwater a short distance to the west of the main town, and it may date from the

Hardy's statue, Dorchester.

57

Lyme Regis.

thirteenth century. Its massive and much altered wall is faced in Portland stone, giving protection to the tiny harbour behind. Until ships grew too large, this was the only safe haven between the Exe and Portland Harbour. Today it is used by fishing and pleasure craft. The Cobb and Lyme Regis feature in Jane Austen's *Persuasion* and John Fowles's *The French Lieutenant's Woman.* To the west of the Cobb is Monmouth Beach, where the Duke of Monmouth landed in 1685. Twelve local men were hanged here after the battle of Sedgemoor.

One can walk from the Cobb to the town centre along the Esplanade, which has an attractive terrace of bow-windowed houses. The focus of the town is where the river Lim enters the sea. Here, at the bottom of Broad Street, is the late Victorian Town Hall and the museum (chapter 7). The parish church (St Michael) is close and has Norman work within a later fabric. There is a memorial window to Mary Anning, the famous fossiler of the early nineteenth century. Dinosaurland in Coombe Street is another reminder of the importance of fossils here. The steep and attractive Broad Street ascends the west side of Lyme Regis. It is mainly Georgian, including the bow-fronted Three Cups Hotel. Further up there are some large villas, such as Belmont at the corner of Pound Street and Cobb Road. Eleanor Coade lived here after 1790, and the house has examples of Coade-stone decoration. Amazingly, the ascent continues just as steeply towards the Devon border.

The Ware Cliffs below this part of Lyme are part of a huge landslipped area which extends into Devon. A big slip in 1839 involved 40 acres (16 ha) of cliff. All is now thickly wooded and of great scientific interest. East of Lyme Regis is the Black Venn, a huge slumping cliff of marls above a beach. This is an important place for fossil collecting. Beyond is Charmouth.

MILTON ABBAS

This is possibly Dorset's best known village. In 1771-90 Joseph Damer (later the Earl of Dorchester) chose to create a park around his house by removing the market town which had lain close to Milton Abbey. The result was the building of this model village, out of sight in a sheltered valley. The gently curving street descends between nearly identical thatched white cottages. Each was built as a pair of cottages with a common front entrance. The village includes the brick and stone almshouses of 1674, taken down from their original site and re-erected here in 1779. The church (St James) dates from 1786.

From the bottom of the street, there is a walk through Capability Brown's landscaped park to the abbey church (chapter 6). Traces of the old town are visible under the grassy slope on the right. The rectangular Milton Abbey House was built in the 1770s. It is now open to the public during the holidays (chapter 5). There is a good first view of the abbey from the Hilton road, while the most pleasant approach to the village is up the gentle valley from Milborne St Andrew. At the top of the village is the Park Farm Museum (chapter 7)

Milton Abbas.

and the Rare Poultry, Pig and Plant Centre is just to the south-west (chapter 8).

OKEFORD FITZPAINE

A good Dorset village, notable for its cottages in a great variety of materials, such as flint, stone, brick, timber and cob, with thatching too, Okeford Fitzpaine lies at a crossroads of lanes in the south-east corner of the Blackmoor Vale, overshadowed by a spur of the chalk escarpment of the Dorset Downs, Okeford Hill. This commands fine views northwards over the village and beyond. In the village centre is the base of a market cross, and a small building houses an eighteenth-century fire engine. The church (St Andrew) is on a low rise a little out of the centre, to the south-east. Apart from the fifteenth-century tower, much of the rest was restored in the mid nineteenth century. The nearby village of Shillingstone, strung out along the A357, is not without interest.

OSMINGTON

Despite the A353, busy with Weymouth-bound summer traffic, there are some interesting stone buildings in this village. For example, the since altered Charity Farm is a late sixteenth-century long-house, where animals were once kept at one end of the farmhouse. Much of the church (St Osmund) was rebuilt in 1846. A lane to the south-east leads down a deep valley to the sea, where there are cottages and an inn. This is Osmington Mills, well known for its lobsters. John Constable spent his honeymoon here and did some painting, including the view of Weymouth Bay.

POOLE
Early closing Wednesday.

Poole is a prosperous modern town and resort, but most interest lies in the old town. At the expense of Wareham, a town and port were developed in the thirteenth century on a peninsula on the north shore of Poole Harbour. Poole merchants, with a long tradition of seafaring, came to specialise in the prosperous Newfoundland trade in the seventeenth and eighteenth centuries. The port is still active, as well as being a major sailing centre. There is always something to see from The Quay, including yachts, ships, tugs and repair yards. Ferry craft leave here for Brownsea Island or circuits of Poole Harbour. At the west end, Poole Bridge opens to allow vessels through. Formerly, there were ships for the disused power station, which is such a landmark. Off West Quay Road is the headquarters of the Royal National Lifeboat Institution, with a museum (chapter 7).

At the east end of The Quay, Poole Pottery is open to visitors (chapter 8). Along the Quay there are many interesting buildings and inns,

59

mostly associated with the shipping industry. Tourist attractions include galleries, restaurants and The Natural World (chapter 8). The Custom House has curved outside steps. Dating from the late eighteenth century, it was rebuilt after a fire in 1813. In front is a replica of the Town Beam — the original weighing and measuring instrument. Two museums are here, Scaplen's Court and the Waterfront, the latter in a warehouse and old stone woolhouse (chapter 7).

This is the place to step into the quiet streets behind the bustle of The Quay. Thames Street leads quickly to the early nineteenth-century St James's Church. Within, pine pillars are a reminder of the Newfoundland trade. There are some fine merchants' houses around the church, but the humbler Church Street is also pleasant. This has almshouses, built at the time of Henry V and purchased for the Corporation in 1550. Market Street has the Guildhall of 1761, now a museum (chapter 7), while Market Close has Sir Peter Thompson's House (1746), which is considered to be the best in the town. The lower part of the long High Street has most interest, as it approaches The Quay.

The old town is overwhelmed by later developments. The Borough of Poole extends eastwards to Bournemouth, and it includes Parkstone and Sandbanks. The latter forms a peninsula at the northern side of the entrance to Poole Harbour, and a chain ferry provides a crossing to Studland. In summer the queues for the ferry are almost matched by hundreds of sailing craft navigating the narrows. At Canford Cliffs are Compton Acres Gardens (chapter 5).

PORTESHAM

This is an inviting village of pale limestone houses, at a springhead below steep hills, about 2 miles (3 km) east of Abbotsbury. The church (St Peter) is mostly of the fifteenth century, but with some evidence for an earlier structure. The seventeenth-century manor was the home of Admiral Hardy of Trafalgar fame, and a bridleway leads from the village to his monument on Black Down, 1 mile (1.6 km) north-east (see chapter 2). To the east, the lane to Upwey follows the foot of a ridge before crossing it through a narrow gap. Along the way notable buildings are passed at Waddon Manor and Friar Waddon.

POWERSTOCK

This is a small attractive village of stone cottages scattered around a hillside and lost among the deep valleys of west Dorset. There are traces of field systems outside the village, and the earthworks of a Norman motte and bailey, sited on a spur between two streams. See chapter 6 for the church.

SHAFTESBURY

Early closing Wednesday, market day Thursday.

Shaftesbury is a small but busy market town, standing at 700 feet (213 m) above sea level on a greensand spur overlooking the Blackmoor Vale. There was an existing Saxon settlement in AD 880, when King Alfred founded an abbey, but little remains of this once great building at Park Walk (chapter 7).

Gold Hill is Shaftesbury's showpiece and is much loved by film makers. It is a steep cobbled street with old cottages on one side and the buttressed precinct wall of the abbey on the other, all set against a backdrop of pure Dorset countryside. At the top is the museum (chapter 7) and the back of the crenellated Town Hall of 1826. Next to this in the High Street is St Peter's church with its solid greensand tower. It is mainly of the fifteenth and sixteenth centuries and has some interesting carvings on the side facing the High Street. Within, the church has been carefully repaired after being allowed to fall into decay. Holy Trinity church, whose tower stands high above the spur, dates from 1841 and is now a community centre. The Grosvenor Hotel is a late eighteenth-century coaching inn and is noted for its elaborately carved Chevy Chase sideboard. Away from the shops there are thatched cottages in the smaller Bell Street.

The wide Park Walk gives excellent views across the Blackmoor Vale. Below is St James village, with thatched cottages and an attractive group around a pump yard. The earthworks of the abbey fishponds lie at the valley head. On the north side of the spur, Castle Hill provides views to the Mendips, Glastonbury Tor and Quantock Hills. The site of the castle at the end of the spur has little to show. The village below is Enmore Green, from which Shaftesbury once obtained its water. The annual Byzant Ceremony ensured the right of the hilltop town to take water from here. The Byzant, a form of decorated mace, was carried and a pair of gloves, a gallon of ale and a calf's head were presented to the Lord of the Manor. The ceremony has lapsed but in modern times an annual Gold Hill Fair is held on the first full weekend in July.

SHERBORNE

Early closing Wednesday, market day Thursday.

Good houses of golden brown stone give this market town an air of authority. It is best known for its abbey church (chapter 6) and its schools. The present Sherborne School was founded in 1550, probably on an earlier site, and former abbey buildings are incorporated on the north side of the church. The fifteenth-century monks' Guesten Hall is now the library, the Abbot's Hall is the school chapel,

Shaftesbury Abbey.

and there is also the abbey kitchen, all within a complex of later school buildings. Across the green from the abbey church, at the corner of Half Moon Street, is the Almshouse of St John the Baptist and St John the Evangelist, begun in 1437 for twelve men and four women. A Victorian extension is fully in keeping with this lovely stone building. The almshouse chapel dates from 1442 and contains paintings of the same century and good woodwork.

A walk through the streets around the central part of Sherborne is rewarding for the great variety of houses. Cheap Street is the main shopping street, with the Conduit forming a focal point at its lower end. This was not a market cross but was salvaged from the abbey cloisters, where it had been built as a lavatory by Abbot Mere (1504-35). The town's museum (chapter 7) is just behind, opposite timber-framed buildings in a walkway to the abbey church. Further up Cheap Street is the late sixteenth-century timber-framed Abbey-lands, with three gables and additions of 1649. There are Georgian houses of note around the Green at the top of the street, where the A30 passes through, luckily avoiding the centre. Look in the side streets, such as Abbey Street with its eighteenth-century Abbey House, and Hospital Lane with the unusual Abbey Grange, which was converted from part of the old tithe barn. Newlands has Lord Digby's School, a tall building of about 1720. This is considered one of the finest buildings in Sherborne and was designed by Benjamin Bastard. Long Street, opposite the Conduit, has notable houses including the Red House of 1730. This is of red brick, with some stone

details, and is set back from the thoroughfare. Long Street leads east to Castleton and the old and new castles (chapters 4 and 5). In Castleton, Dorset's largest surviving waterwheel is being restored in a building where it pumped Sherborne's water supply for nearly a hundred years.

Sherborne comes alive for the traditional Pack Monday Fair, which takes place on the first Monday after the 10th October. It dates back to the time when the builders were paid off upon completion of the abbey.

STALBRIDGE

This is a long village on the edge of the Blackmoor Vale, with the A357 passing through the narrow High Street. Many of the stone houses are of local Forest marble. Much of the medieval market cross survives in a weathered condition, although the crucifixion is a more recent addition. The church (St Mary) was rebuilt in the second half of the nineteenth century, but fourteenth-century piers with carved capitals are of interest. It lies a little removed at the north end of the village where the extensive wall around Stalbridge Park is a prominent feature. The early seventeenth-century house was demolished in 1822, but a rustic-styled stone gateway remains beside the main road. At the south end of the village the road divides at The Ring, where there are attractive nineteenth-century estate cottages. The Somerset and Dorset Railway passed the village, and the site of the former station is now a small industrial area.

STURMINSTER NEWTON

Early closing Wednesday, market day Monday.

The town is built on a spur of higher ground within a meander of the river Stour. Mondays are busy when its large market is open. This serves the Blackmoor Vale and is England's largest calf market. The old Market Place has been partly infilled, but it still retains the base of a cross. The best houses are in the quiet back streets, such as Penny Street, where brick and yellow Marnhull stone are the most common materials. The church (St Mary) is of greensand but is disappointing after a Victorian rebuilding. A criss-cross pattern on the tower is unusual. It is somewhat removed from the town centre, overlooking meadows and the Stour. The poet William Barnes attended the old school here, and a carved lectern in the church is a memorial to him. Thomas Hardy lived at Riverside in 1876-8. This overlooks an island in the Stour on the west side of town. The museum is in Bath Road, on the north side (chapter 7).

To the south, the Stour is crossed by a medieval bridge of six arches. In common with many Dorset bridges, there is a cast iron sign warning that anyone damaging the bridge will be liable to transportation for life. Opposite the bridge is the so-called 'Castle', a manor house within possible iron age defences. Just upstream is Sturminster Newton Mill, beside a large weir (chapter 8). The village of Newton has timber-framed and thatched houses. About 1 mile (1.6 km) north of the town is Hinton St Mary, where a Roman mosaic was discovered in 1963.

SWANAGE

Early closing Thursday.

Swanage is a mainly nineteenth-century resort, set on the sandy sweep of Swanage Bay between Peveril Point and the high chalk cliffs of Ballard Point. The railway came late, in 1885, and Bournemouth steamers called regularly at the now disused pier. Church Hill is an attractive survivor of the old settlement, with a pond and stone cottages surrounded by later developments. The Tithe Barn Museum is here too (chapter 7). Before tourism, the town was an important centre for Purbeck stone and marble, which was quarried and mined extensively on the hills and coast to the south. Large quantities were shipped from Swanage, where there were masons' yards along the seafront.

The town is associated with John Mowlem and his nephew George Burt, who became contractors in London and founded the Mowlem group, which now comprises fifty companies. They influenced their home town in a fascinating way, by bringing back unusual materials as ballast in returning stone ships. The Town Hall in the High Street dates from the 1880s but has the elaborately carved seventeenth-century entrance of the Mercers' Hall, Cheapside. Just up the road is Purbeck House, built by Burt in 1875. It is an extrava-

LEFT: *The Great Globe at Durlston Park, Swanage.*
RIGHT: *The Town Hall at Swanage has an elaborate front, salvaged from the Mercers' Hall, Cheapside.*

ganza incorporating many interesting relics and architectural details from London. It is now a convent. On the seafront, the modern Mowlem Theatre is on the site of the Mowlem Institute of 1863. A granite column surmounted by four cannonballs was erected by John Mowlem in 1862, to commemorate King Alfred's victory against the Danish fleet in AD 877, although the notorious Peveril Ledge is believed to have caused the destruction of the fleet. The clock tower near the lifeboat station once stood at the south end of London Bridge as a memorial to Wellington. George Burt re-erected it (minus clock) at Swanage in 1868. Around the town, several inscribed lamp posts and bollards clearly came from London.

The railway station is the centre of the preserved Swanage Railway, which is being reopened to Corfe Castle and Wareham (chapter 8). South of the town is Durlston Head, with Burt's Durlston Castle. Below, is his 10 foot (3 m) diameter Great Globe of Portland stone, erected in 1887. The Head and clifftop paths are included in the Durlston Country Park (chapter 2).

SYDLING ST NICHOLAS

This neat village lies in the chalk valley of the Sydling Water. The grouping of unassuming cottages in the main street gives the village its charm. The church (St Nicholas) is set apart from the village, on higher ground. It was rebuilt in the fifteenth and eighteenth centuries. Outside, there are some fine gargoyles. Plain glass windows give light to the interior, where eighteenth- and nineteenth-century wall monuments are numerous. Next to the church, the Court House is of the eighteenth and nineteenth centuries. On the other side, the farm has a tithe barn, unfortunately with a corrugated iron roof. As with the parallel Cerne Valley, there are many field systems on the surrounding slopes. These include the earthworks of a middle bronze age farming settlement on Shearplace Hill.

WAREHAM

Early closing Wednesday.

Wareham was once a significant port at the gateway to Purbeck, until eclipsed by Poole in the thirteenth century. The town's earlier history is associated with attacks by the Danes. It was one of King Alfred's strongly defended Saxon burhs, and massive ramparts still survive between the rivers Frome and Piddle. Little remains of the later Norman castle. The present town is mainly of brick and Georgian in appearance, because of a fire in 1762. The planned street pattern centres on the main North, South, West and East Streets. A sculpted black bear outside the inn of that name catches the eye in South Street. At the crossroads, the Victorian Town Hall has a corner clock tower and thin spire and is in stark contrast to the earlier buildings. Behind, in East Street, is the musuem (chapter 7). Opposite this are the almshouses, which have a belfry and the cupola from the eighteenth-century town hall.

Wareham has two important churches. The tiny St Martin's church, beside the former north gate, has Saxon origins and dates mainly from the eleventh century. There are wall paintings and a white marble effigy of T. E. Lawrence in Arab dress, by Eric Kennington. Lawrence, who lived at Clouds Hill, had taken an interest in the restoration of this church. The tower of Lady St Mary's church is an important landmark behind the quay on the Frome. Inside, the old Saxon church was much altered in the nineteenth century. There are inscriptions of the sixth or seventh centuries, pre-dating the Saxons, and a boat-shaped stone coffin, said to have contained the body of King Edward the Martyr after his murder at Corfe in AD 978, before being transferred to Shaftesbury Abbey. The church has the only hexagonal leaden font in England. It has the figures of the twelve Apostles on its sides and dates from the twelfth century. Two thirteenth-century effigies represent former governors of Wareham Castle. John Hutchins, the eighteenth-century Dorset historian, was rector here and is commemorated in the east window. Behind the church is the Tudor Priory. Wareham's third church (Holy Church) is now an art gallery at the end of South Street near the Frome bridge. The old quay, with its eighteenth-century brick granary, is a popular focal point here. There are riverside walks towards Poole Harbour.

WEYMOUTH

Early closing Wednesday.

Weymouth is a fine resort, with much of interest. The Romans had a port at the head of Radipole Lake, but it was not until the thirteenth century that Melcombe Regis and Weymouth were created as new towns on the north and south sides of the harbour. Fame as a bathing resort came to Melcombe Regis in the later eighteenth century. This brought the Duke of Gloucester, who built a house (now part of the Gloucester Hotel) in 1780 and persuaded his brother George III to go nine years later. The king returned several times, to the great benefit of the town. He is commemorated by a huge stone plinth and a painted statue of Coade stone, erected by the grateful inhabitants in the fiftieth year of his reign. This stands on the sea front, before the bowed ends of two Georgian terraces.

The gentle curve of the beach and esplanade is best seen from the harbour pier with its modern pavilion. There are fine Georgian terraces, including the balconied Assembly

Rooms, latterly a yacht club. Further north, past the Gloucester Hotel, the terraces are Victorian. The colourful Jubilee Clock (1887) is conspicuous on the esplanade. Further along the shore, attractions in the Lodmoor Country Park include the Sea Life Centre and the Weymouth Butterfly Farm (chapter 8).

Within the older part of the town, the narrow medieval street pattern is preserved. The Georgian church of St Mary (1815-17) has a short clock tower and cupola; and was built to serve the fashionable folk of the period. The railway reached the town in 1857, which ensured its success as a resort. A new Channel Islands ferry service was inaugurated, and in 1865 rails were laid along the quay to the terminus near the harbour mouth. The harbour is bustling with boats and always a source of interest. Several quayside warehouses have been converted for the holiday trade and one is the Deep Sea Adventure and Shipwreck Centre (chapter 7).

The original town of Weymouth is reached by the Town Bridge, or by a rowing boat service from near the ferry terminal. The old Town Hall looks more like a small chapel in the High Street, which is up the hill behind the modern council offices. Tudor House is in Trinity Street (chapter 5). The former Weymouth Brewery in Hope Square is to become a museum complex. There are many pleasing terraces in the back streets hereabouts. Nothe Gardens are laid out south of the harbour entrance, and there are good views of the town, Weymouth Bay and the Portland Breakwater. The nineteenth-century Nothe Fort is at the end of the promontory (chapter 4).

Modern Weymouth has expanded into large suburbs incorporating Melcombe Regis and former villages, for example Wyke Regis, where the churchyard has burials from shipwrecks on Chesil Beach. Upwey has old mills and a famous wishing well (chapter 8), where George III used a gold cup which later became the Ascot Gold Cup. The king has a lasting memorial at Sutton Poyntz, to the north-east of Weymouth. This is a figure of the king on horseback, cut into the chalk hillside in 1815 and visible from the town.

WIMBORNE MINSTER
Early closing Wednesday.

The older part of Wimborne Minster lies in a small area between the rivers Allen and Stour, over which were once important bridges. The town's main interest is the twin towered minster, which may be on the site of a Saxon nunnery (chapter 6). Today the town centre is still able to hold its identity against encroaching suburbs to the south and east, and its bypass has greatly eased traffic problems in its narrow streets. Brick has been used in many of the eighteenth- and nineteenth-century buildings which give the town its main appeal, especially in the Square, High Street and West Borough. This last, which leads north from the centre, has some of the best Georgian buildings. In the northern outskirts is the new Walford Mill Craft Centre. The Priest's House Museum is in the High Street, and its external appearance of the seventeenth or eighteenth century hides the fact that its interior may date from about 1500 (chapter 7). Deans Court Garden and the Walford Mill Craft Centre are also in the town, with Merley Bird Gardens and House nearby (chapters 5, 7 and 8).

WOOL

The village lies on slightly higher ground, just south of the river Frome, with its old bridge and manor house (chapter 9). The modern railway station and level crossing are probably the most remembered features, and the huge nuclear establishment at Winfrith Heath is not far away. However, the old part of the village is passed through on the road to Lulworth Cove, and there are some points of interest for those with time to stop. The church (Holy Rood) is off-centre on the east side of the village. It was much rebuilt in 1864-5, but there is some thirteenth-century work and a squat tower of the fifteenth century. A very fine late medieval altar frontal, made from vestments, is in the County Museum at Dorchester. To the east, the ruins of Bindon Abbey are privately owned by the Weld Estate.

YETMINSTER

Low-lying, to the south-west of Sherborne, Yetminster offers fine examples of stone architecture, especially of the seventeenth century. A walk through the village is therefore greatly rewarded. The church (St Andrew) is mainly of the mid-fifteenth century, although the long chancel is of two centuries earlier. Among the monuments, note the Horsey family brass of 1531. Sir Robert Boyle's School was built in the village in 1697. Yetminster is on the railway from Yeovil to Dorchester but appears little affected on account of its proximity to Yeovil. The neighbouring villages of Beer Hackett and Ryme Intrinseca have their greatest interest in their names.

11
Tourist information centres

Blandford Forum: Marsh and Ham Car Park, West Street, Blandford Forum DT11 7AW. Telephone: 0258 451989.
Bournemouth: Westover Road, Bournemouth BH1 2BU. Telephone: 0202 291715 or 290883.
Bridport: 32 South Street, Bridport DT6 3NQ. Telephone: 0308 24901.
Christchurch: 30 Saxon Square, Christchurch BH23 1QB. Telephone: 0202 471780.
Dorchester: 7 Acland Road, Dorchester DT1 1EF. Telephone: 0305 67992.
Lyme Regis: The Guildhall, Bridge Street, Lyme Regis DT7 3QA. Telephone: 02974 2138.
Poole: Enefco House, Poole Quay, Poole BH15 1HE. Telephone: 0202 673322.
Portland: St George's Centre, Reforne, Portland DT5 2AN. Telephone: 0305 823406.
St Leonards: Camper Information Centre, adjacent to A31, Avon Forest Park. Telephone: 0425 478470. Closed in winter.
Shaftesbury: Bell Street, Shaftesbury SP7 8AE. Telephone: 0747 53514.
Sherborne: Hound Street, Sherborne DT9 3AA. Telephone: 0935 815341.
Swanage: Shore Road, Swanage BH19 1LB. Telephone: 0929 422885.
Wareham: Town Hall, East Street, Wareham BH20 4NS. Telephone: 09295 2740.
Wimborne Minster: 29 High Street, Wimborne Minster BH21 1LB. Telephone: 0202 886116.

DORSET

Legend:

* Nature reserve, viewpoint, picnic area etc. (Ch.2)
ㄇ Archaeological site (Ch.3)
c Castle or fortification (Ch.4)
▲ Historic house, garden (Ch.5)
+ Church (Ch.6)
M Museum (Ch.7)
O Other place of interest (Ch.8)
H Thomas Hardy association (Ch.9)
■ Town or village (Ch.10)

WINCANTON ●

Silton

GILLINGHAM ■M

Dorset Rare Breeds Centre O
and Farm Museum

R.Stour

Sandford
Orcas Manor ▲

Trent +

H
Marnhull +

■ Stalbridge

STURMIN
NEWTO
H M

Fiddlefor
Mill Hous ▲

Okeford ■
Fitzpaine

YEOVIL ●

O
Worldwide
Butterflies

M ■ SHERBORNE
C ▲

BLACKMOOR VALE

Mill O

■ Yetminster

● CHARD

● CREWKERNE

* Winyard's Gap

+ Melbury Bubb

Bulbarrow
ㄇ * Hill

Forde ▲
Abbey

Broadwindsor
O Craft Centre

Evershot H

Batcombe

Minterne
Gdns ▲
* H

+ Buckland
Newton

Hilton

▲ Miltc
+ Abb

ㄇ * Pilsdon Pen
Parnham ▲
House

■ Beaminster

Nettlecombe ㄇ Melcombe
Tout Horsey +

Cerne ▲
Giant

H Plush

Rare Poultry, O
Pigs and Plant Mi
Centre Ab

■ M
Mi

Mapperton
Gardens

Cattistock ■

Cerne Abbas ■ ㄇ

Sydling
St.Nicholas
+ Maiden
Newton

H Piddletrenthide

Deverel ┌
Barrow

MARSHWOOD
VALE
+ Whitchurch
Canonicorum

Toller Fratrum +

+ ■ Powerstock

ㄇ Eggardon Hill

H Puddletown

▲ M

Dinosaurland
M O ■ Charmouth
LYME
REGIS
Golden
Cap

Chideock ●

M ■ BRIDPORT

Burton Bradstock

M

ㄇ

ㄇ

ㄇ Nine
Stones

Athelhampton
Charminster H Higher
* Wolfeton * Bockhampton
▲ House
H Stinsford

Tolpuddle

Cloud
Hill

DORCHESTER
M ■ H

R.Frome

ㄇ Maiden + Whitcombe
Castle

Mill House ■
M Working
Cider Muse

* Hardy
Monument

ㄇ South Dorset Ridgeway

* ㄇ ㄇ

■ Portesham

Abbotsbury
▲ O

Sutton
H Poyntz H Poxwell

Duro
ㄇ Doc
*

CHESIL BEACH

Upwey Mill and
Wishing Well

Jordan Hill ㄇ

■ Osmington

Lulwo
Co

O Lodmoor Country
Park

H
M ■ WEYMOUTH
C

C Sandsfoot Castle

M C Portland Castle
● C * Verne Citadel
Fortuneswell H M ISLE OF PORTLAND
C Rufus
Castle

* Portland Bill

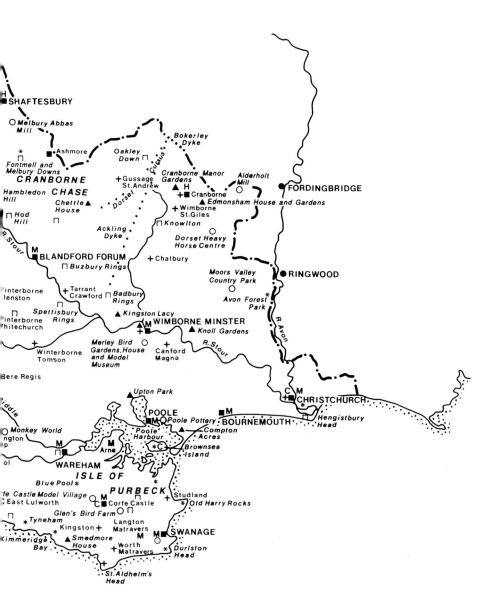

H SHAFTESBURY

○ *Melbury Abbas Mill*

* ■ Ashmore
Oakley Down

Fontmell and Melbury Downs

CRANBORNE + *Gussage St.Andrew*

Hambledon Hill **CHASE**

Chettle ▲ House

□ *Hod Hill*

□

Ackling Dyke

M ■ BLANDFORD FORUM
□ *Buzbury Rings*

interborne lenston + *Tarrant Crawford* □ *Badbury Rings*

Spettisbury Rings
interborne hitechurch

+ *Winterborne Tomson*

Bere Regis

Bokerley Dyke

Cranborne Manor Gardens
▲ **H**
■ Cranborne

+ *Wimborne St.Giles*

□ Knowlton

Dorset Heavy Horse Centre ○

+ *Chalbury*

Alderholt Mill ○

● FORDINGBRIDGE

▲ *Edmonsham House and Gardens*

Moors Valley Country Park ○

● RINGWOOD

* *Avon Forest Park*

▲ *Kingston Lacy* ▲ M **WIMBORNE MINSTER**
▲ *Knoll Gardens*

Merley Bird Gardens,House and Model Museum ○ + *Canford Magna*

R. Stour

R. Avon

R. Stour

Upton Park

□ *Monkey World* ○
ngton p

ol

M □ **WAREHAM**
M ▲ *Arne*

■ M ● POOLE
M○ *Poole Pottery* ■ M **BOURNEMOUTH**
Poole Harbour
* C
▲ *Compton Acres*
Brownsea Island

C M **CHRISTCHURCH**
■ *Hengistbury Head*
*

ISLE OF

Blue Pool *

PURBECK

fe Castle Model Village ○ M
East Lulworth C ■ *Corfe Castle*

Glen's Bird Farm ○ □

* *Tyneham*
Kingston +
Langton Matravers

imeridge Bay ▲ *Smedmore House*

+ *Worth Matravers*

Studland
* *Old Harry Rocks*

M ○ **SWANAGE**
* *Durlston Head*

St.Aldhelm's Head

Index